'Through intimate conversations with remarkable CEOs, Georgie uncovers the "secret sauce recipe" that defines their paths to greatness. This book is a treasure trove of wisdom, offering valuable insights into how these leaders have built exceptional teams, fostered thriving company cultures, and inspired their workforce to achieve unparalleled success. *Stratospheric CEOs* is a captivating journey that will leave you empowered to reach new heights in your own leadership journey. Georgie has masterfully crafted a book that not only captures the essence of extraordinary leadership, but also provides a roadmap for anyone aspiring to create a lasting impact in their professional and personal lives.'

— **Dr Marshall Goldsmith**, Thinkers50 #1 executive coach and *New York Times* bestselling author of *The Earned Life, Triggers* and *What Got You Here Won't Get You There*

'In this book, Georgie Dickins has developed a unique perspective into the decision-making strategies of highly innovative CEOs.'

— **Bill Ford**, Chairman and Chief Executive Officer, General Atlantic

STRATO
SPHERIC
CEOs

Inspirational
real-world lessons
in leadership for the
modern-day
leader

Georgie Dickins

Re**think**

First published in Great Britain in 2024
by Rethink Press (www.rethinkpress.com)

Contents

Introduction

Are you wondering whether this book is for you? The answer's simple. It is for the leader you could be.

You may have an unwavering belief that the world is yours for the taking. That positive mindset means you are ready to create, to grow and to lead. In which case, please read on.

You may already be working within a business or have founded one of your own. You may be sitting in an empty room with only a laptop and your dreams. Wherever you are in your life right now, your self-belief, desire and ambition can take you places, whether that's from the shop floor to the C-suite, or from the boardroom to the rarefied atmosphere of the professional stratosphere.

Do you want to grasp opportunities? To develop your business and yourself? To innovate and adapt? To self-discover? To think differently to the rest of the herd? To learn from those who have been there and achieved their ambitious goals?

You may want to revolutionise an industry, disrupt existing technologies, build a new business or simply grow within one. You may have a great idea or a passionate commitment to self-development. You may be prepared to go outside your comfort zone, to do the unexpected, to think in new ways. Ultimately, you may just want to do things better, to trust in a process and to fulfil your potential.

If you want neuroscientific analysis and statistics about the benefits of an Ivy League education, look away, now! This is not an academic study – you won't find quotes from professors or vast tracts of university research theses. This book isn't about theory;

there isn't an equation or an MBA in sight. It is, however, full of golden nuggets of practical advice, insight and wisdom from people who have been there and done it. Those who have taken the mesmeric leap into the stratosphere and converted their dreams into reality.

Advice from the stratosphere

This is a book about leadership. It will help you lead anything – from a small team through to a multinational, and any venture in between.

How you show up influences how people experience you. The insights in these pages provide a guide on how to show up as a *stratospheric* leader. This is a term I use to describe visionary thinkers. It sums up the level at which they operate; the rarefied atmosphere that few get to inhabit, because breathing thin air isn't easy. It puts pressure on the body and the senses.

The people featured in this book are leaders who have reached the stratosphere. Transformation is at the heart of everything they do. They have achieved the Mars mission goals, authoring their own multibillion-dollar growth strategies and creating enduring, world-leading businesses. They are people who have the ability to foresee future opportunities and trends, to identify unmet needs and to create solutions for them.

I have the good fortune to call these people my friends and they have become the most incredible advocates. During our conversations, I was humbled by their candour and the time they invested in passing on their wisdom. They opened up about their lives, the lessons they've learned, the mistakes they've made, all in a desire to enable others to learn from their journeys. It has been a privilege spending time with them.

Even though they are individuals I have known for many years, I confess I came into this project with preconceived ideas about the leaders I interviewed. Thoughts filled my head of tunnel vision, ruthlessness, perhaps even an albeit understandable selfishness as they strived to reach their goals. I assumed due to their busyness, they would show up distracted, preoccupied and short on time.

I couldn't have been more wrong.

What I learned were their 'human skills', their abilities to deftly balance their relentless ambition with empathy and warmth. I was surprised by their generosity (both of time and of themselves) and the dynamic exuberance that they displayed. Their energy, positivity and desire to engage with me meaningfully were infectious and invigorating. I left every conversation a different person to the one who went in. Their stories catalysed my thinking and inspired me to continue to refine and follow my own audacious goals. Put simply, they gave me a masterclass in building followership and leadership.

Although each leader profiled in this book has their own unique blend of skills and qualities, there were golden threads that ran between them all, and these are the focus of the chapters that make up Part One. A core theme running across all seven chapters is 'raising the bar', which one of our CEOs describes as the gold standard way of saying, 'I want everything to be incrementally better'.

When it comes to people, strategy, execution – these leaders have an ethos of continuous learning; always pushing the edges of what is possible. They are looking for success in every part of the journey and they never give up raising their game to the next level.

When I started working (decades ago now!), I imagined that great leadership was all about inspiring speeches, an aggressive work rate and an eye constantly focused on the bottom line. As I moved upwards and came into ever-closer contact with the people at the apex of organisations, I recognised the value and importance they placed on the human side of leadership. I became intrigued by the mindset, behaviours and strategies of these leaders. The more I immersed myself, the more fascinated I became, which ultimately led to my own career move.

Now in the second act of my career, as a coach and trusted advisor to global leaders, I have the great fortune to be invited behind the curtain. I get to see what they do and how they do it. I have learned their critical lessons, and one key learning is that their impact, their influence, their fulfilment in life is by design.

I want this book to democratise leadership and make the lessons and learnings from the industry titans available to all. They are not my lessons – they are the ones stratospheric leaders have shared. My role has been to create the space, to ask the incisive questions and tease out the insights and lessons that have the most value. My overlay merely builds on the lessons, as well as offering thoughts and suggestions on how to apply the learnings.

Why *these* CEOs?

I spent twenty years of my career working in fintech, and founder CEOs have played a key part in revolutionising an industry I was part of. The CEOs in this book are people I had the privilege of meeting during my career in financial services and I was always really fascinated by the founder-CEO combination – those with transformative ideas combined with an ability to build businesses. It is one thing to have the seed of an idea and it is quite another to turn it into a world-leading business.

I was intentional about the interviewees for this book: founder CEOs in fintech who have created multibillion-dollar businesses; those at the cutting edge, applying technology. These are people who think differently. They are disruptors who operate with incredible confidence and diligence, and have the skill, instinct and enterprising mindset to do so. They are people who have stayed the course with relentless perseverance and unwavering conviction and faith. There is an obsession in what they do, what one might almost term a crazy level of dedication. To find them still at the helm decades later speaks of the value they have created, their love for what they do and the continuing followership they have cultivated.

It's important to acknowledge the obvious fact that there are no women represented among the stratospheric CEOs featured in the book, which in part was a key driver for me personally to become its author. By drawing together these stories, I can provide support and insights for the women in this ecosystem who are the next generation of leaders and builders of multibillion-dollar businesses.

There is one exception to the founder-CEO filter, Chris Willcox. His career affords us a unique viewpoint of – and additional context around – each of the fintech founders. He has, at different stages, been a customer, a user, a counterparty stakeholder, a board member and a partner in Tradeweb, MarketAxess, Intercapital Brokers (ICAP), Morgan Stanley Capital International (MSCI) and IHS Markit. He is not only an incredibly successful and accomplished leader in his own right, but also one of the most inspiring people I have had the privilege of working for.

How to use this book

Stratospheric CEOs is divided into two parts, 'Lessons Learned' and 'How To Apply The Learnings'. You can, of course, read from the start to the finish, or you may want to dive into a specific chapter. Equally, you may see where the page falls open. Each time you pick up this book, it is my hope that it teaches you something new, sparks you or provokes your thinking – or maybe all three.

Although the leaders profiled are from fintech, the leadership lessons they share are universal and can equally be applied in other sectors. You will find the lessons digestible, tactical and practical. Before we dive into the chapters, I have first shared mini bios of each CEO as a way to introduce you to them individually and give you a sense of who they are when they are not in the stratospheric CEO seat – their human side.

Part One details the invaluable lessons these CEOs have shared with me over the course of our conversations. In Part Two, you will find a distillation of the insight emails I share with my clients. When I started writing this book, I was keen to get a sense of the lessons that truly landed with people while flexing my own writing skills, so I put myself into my discomfort zone and launched a weekly 'Insights and Inspiration from the Stratosphere' blog. I have taken a selection of these insight emails to build on the material covered in Part One and support you in applying the learnings.

Finally, the Appendix shares some of my favourite quotes and soundbites from the stratospheric CEOs featured throughout the book.

I don't advise you to take any of these leaders' approaches in aggregate. Reconcile the insights, cherry pick from their stories and create your own approach and playbook for success. If I have done justice to even a fraction of the wisdom I received on this journey, I am excited for what unfolds for you.

I hope you take as much inspiration from reading the lessons as I did from collecting them.

Meet Our CEOs

Lance Uggla:
Founder and CEO, IHS Markit

If you know fintech, you'll know Lance Uggla as the founder and CEO of IHS Markit, the global diversified provider of critical information, analytics and solutions. Lance's name has become synonymous for vision, drive and success. He appears to have a magical talent for alchemy, but what's more observable about Lance is his humility, down-to-earth nature, personal charisma, nuclear energy and passion for what he does. The pride and love he has for his family is clear, too – whether he is talking about his parents, sister, children or grandchildren, there is such warmth and connection in his words.

If there was anything notable about his upbringing, it was simply an appetite for work. Lance grew up in British Columbia. His dad was a sawmill manager. In that environment, chores were non-negotiable. Many of us consider it a triumph to listen to the news and get dressed before breakfast; the Uggla family would have been out working on their property at the crack of dawn. Every member of the family was expected to lend a hand, and Lance's natural instinct was to lend two.

Lance was always competitive. As a small child, he would push himself to beat his sister at jigsaw challenges. He skipped a grade in school and worked hard to prove himself. From the age of thirteen, he worked a forty-hour week over and above his education. He would race home from school to complete his homework so that he could head to his job, and would then work until the small hours to earn enough money to be self-sufficient.

For Lance, it was simple: work hard, go to school and do well leads to success. His work ethic and love for winning was already beginning to shine through, and he was extolling the virtues of leadership.

This was hugely impressive, of course, but not a fast lane to the stratosphere. He was still a boy from Vancouver attending a local school, working hard to earn some cash, but a solid and stable home environment and the unwavering love of his parents instilled in him confidence and self-belief.

Lance studied business at Simon Fraser University in Canada before moving to the UK in the mid-1980s to study accounting and finance at the London School of Economics (LSE). This was a time when people still used calculators, and Excel was a visionary new advancement in the world of tech. It was also a period of great change and opportunity.

Post university, he went on to work at CIBC and TD Bank in trading roles. During this time, he remembers having an entrepreneurial instinct, seeking out opportunities to create innovative products and looking at ways to use new technologies to gain a competitive advantage. He could see that things were changing in the world around data and regulation: 'The period from 1986 through 2000 was an incredibly steep technology curve, moving from calculators to spreadsheets, to fast relational databases.'

In 2001, the big credit hedge funds and dotcoms were emerging. There was a focus on information services and technology, and that coupled with changes to regulation due to market failures such as the collapse of Enron presented the opening for Lance to take an entrepreneurial leap. He remembers thinking, 'I have a chance to build something myself too,' realising that the combination of technology and big data could give him a substantial advantage in terms of pre-trade decision making. He saw the opportunity to bring transparency alongside decision making to the credit default swap market.

It was a sliding doors moment: stay at the bank and continue moving upwards, or create his own destiny. In 2001, aged thirty-nine, he started Mark-it.Com, which incorporated in 2003.

Lance says, 'I didn't have a clue about the size and scope of what I was creating at the start, but I knew my original idea was needed in financial markets. It had a purpose and an addressable market to target.' He had a belief in his idea and a belief in himself.

Clearly, Lance benefited from his work ethic and timing. He's not alone there, but that only explains part of the story. It was his ability to see the unmet needs in the market, along with the courage to go out on his own, to take the risk in making the decision and not to be afraid of failing, that made the difference.

Having a healthy risk appetite is essential for a stratospheric CEO. Just as Mark-it.Com was becoming established, Lance sensed the bursting of the dotcom bubble. In that moment, he had a choice: would he go back to a bank, or would he pivot?

Unsurprisingly, he chose the latter. Seeing many fail so quickly pushed Lance to get serious early. He became hyper-focused on having a product the market would buy, leading to a rebrand as Markit Partners. The company strategy evolved, marked by the acquisition of several best-of-class companies in line with the original strategy of accurate pricing and transparency for global credit derivatives, cash credit instruments and syndicated loans.

As a well-known and seasoned dealmaker, Markit merged with IHS in 2016, kick-starting Markit's growth trajectory and giving it the necessary firepower to compete with rivals, including Bloomberg and Thomson Reuters. At the end of 2020, Lance was presented with the biggest deal of his career. After two decades, Markit, now merged with IHS, had grown from a dozen employees working from a barn in St Albans to thousands working in offices around the globe. When S&P Global put in a bid for the business, Lance's father (one of his most trusted confidants) told him it would be his tombstone, but despite his father's words, Lance sensed it was an incredibly compelling opportunity. Given the synergies of both businesses, far from being a tombstone, it would be an amazing capstone for this part of his journey. It was a mega-merger, 2020's biggest mergers and acquisitions (M&A) deal, creating a financial data and information powerhouse, valued at a staggering $44 billion.

Given Lance is not one to sit still, what is his next chapter? The entrepreneurial spirit, passion and pursuit that drove the data information market at the start of the information age have been redirected to something equally relevant in the here and now. His new venture, BeyondNetZero, is a climate fund under private equity firm General Atlantic, where he is focusing on energy efficiency, resource conservation and emissions management.

Once again, he has positioned himself front and centre of the cutting edge, underpinned by his passion, enthusiasm and love for what he does. Lance's team shared a mantra he regularly uses – 'raise the bar' – but he doesn't just raise it, he breaks it, remakes it and keeps on pushing it skywards, and that's what he expects of others.

As a serial entrepreneur who has incredible followership, Lance has taken a legion of people on an incredible journey. I for one am super excited to follow his next chapter.

Rick McVey: Founder and Executive Chairman, MarketAxess

Rick McVey is the archetypal Midwest stratospheric success story. His business, MarketAxess, went public within four years of being founded, with a stock value of $11. MKTX trades around $200 at the time of writing, having been as high as $600 at one point. Today, it is the market leader in the electronic trading of US corporate bonds, responsible for 20% of all corporate bond trading volume in the USA.

Rick didn't spend his childhood studying *The Wall Street Journal* and plotting a future in business. He was the all-American boy who loved sports and dreamt of playing professionally. Failing that, he would be a sports agent, providing a pathway to success.

It wasn't that Rick didn't 'get' business – quite the opposite. His father worked in the oil industry and spent his spare time investing in the markets. Like every great dad, he shared his passion with his son. Young Rick might have been fantasising about winning golf tournaments, but his dad told him about the markets. He explained how they worked, he traded in front of his son and Rick absorbed that knowledge.

Rick stayed close to home for his studies. His sports dream wasn't realised, and on graduating from business school, he decided against becoming Ohio's own Jerry Maguire. Instead, he applied to join a bank in his hometown of Cleveland. He was happy there, trading futures, until his futures brokers from the CME floor suggested that he come join them the on the trading floors. That was where the action was.

Rick's first role there was fast paced – a chaotic tornado of energy. One had to work in tune with the team to profit from the rollercoaster ride of the markets. Rick thrived on the velocity of the work and the thrill of the chase. He stayed on the trading floor for eight years.

Rick then left his CME floor brokerage firm, Discount Corporation of New York, and went to work for a giant. At JP Morgan, he worked alongside the titans of the financial ecosphere, allowing him to visualise how his world could be scaled up. He ran the company's North America Futures & Options business and in his self-deprecating Midwestern way, he says he made a 'nice job of it'. Rick swiftly rose to managing director, moved east to New York and took on JP Morgan's Fixed Income Sales business. He built his reputation within the industry as someone you could trust to implement and execute a flawless strategy.

Like so many of the stratospheric leaders I have worked with over the years, Rick carefully and deliberately nurtured his expertise, learning what was going on inside every corner of the labyrinthine finance world. When an opportunity arose, he was in a position to perceive that need, and in 1999 he saw the niche. Rick had an idea for an electronic trading platform for the institutional credit markets that he shared with his colleagues at JP Morgan. He launched MarketAxess as an independent venture in 2000, with backing from JP Morgan and other large banks who saw the enormous potential.

Rick is an opportunist and a visionary, but that doesn't set him apart from our other leaders. If there's a single quality that defines Rick and helps to explain why he is where he is, it's his empathy. He's the ultimate people person.

That has been true from the start. He was incredibly close to his mother, to whom he remained 'Richard' until sadly, she passed in 2019. At school, he demonstrated boundless energy and a knack for getting along with others. He recognised early on that people are attracted to positive energy and has maintained his key mentoring relationships throughout his career. Despite his success, position and wealth, he remains popular with friends inside and away from the world of work.

I have observed Rick at work, where he is unfailingly charismatic. He may be the founder of MarketAxess, a fintech giant worth billions of dollars, but he always remains available to his staff. 'My door's open' is a mantra rolled out by many a business leader, but in practice, the open door leads to a gatekeeper. Not for Rick – his team members know he is there for them, and not just for a chat. If there's a fire, they know he will run into it, fighting it side-by-side with them.

This isn't an act; Rick gets people and always has. He has never turned his back on his Midwestern roots. He was raised in a loving family home by parents who wanted to give their children everything. He has recreated this environment in his adult home, with a wife and three daughters from a previous marriage, whom he adores. This solid family base gives him the easy confidence that he takes with him from the bar to the boardroom, providing him with the ability to operate on a level with the most junior staff member all the way up to the board level. Rick is another stratospheric CEO who attracts people like moths to a flame. He is fun, funny and inspiring. He expects a lot, but he gives back more. He puts his confidence and conviction upfront, even in times of crisis.

Rick is not just there for his own people. He may love his family and care passionately about his colleagues, but it is his ability to put his clients first that has defined his business culture. This focus on people and culture has shaped his entire client-centric business model. While others have grown huge businesses through acquisition, Rick has pursued entirely organic growth. From the first day, he has been unwaveringly consistent with his 'build it and they will come' approach to life – put people first and the rest will follow.

His friends describe him as the salt of the earth, and he seems to be surrounded by friends wherever he goes. He finds it easy to strike up relationships with people he meets, and crowds gather around him. He talks about 'we' not 'I', he always seems to be smiling and he radiates happiness. That's not a coincidence; he structures his life to ensure he stays happy and fit. He plays golf and he works on his physical and mental agility. Life in the stratosphere requires you to manage yourself as well as those around you – Rick gets that, and he maximises his own wellbeing because he knows he will only live once and that smiling is contagious.

Make no mistake, Rick is a great technician. Maths was his thing at school, and it led him to finance. He has a relentless focus on detail and execution. He knows that whatever tomorrow brings, there will always be another opportunity, another strategy, another prospect. He has a vision and the agility to change direction as the world changes – and often before.

Had he become a sports agent, Rick would have fitted the Jerry Maguire model: authentic, altruistic and amiable. As it is, even though sport has remained in his life merely as a hobby, Rick has made winning a habit throughout his professional career and he's done it thoughtfully, calmly and methodically.

When asked what critical lessons he learned as he climbed the ladder, Rick responded, 'You are best taking one job at a time. Nobody is born a CEO. You build a career with strong foundations with great people around you.'

That is the fundamental thing for Rick: people. Not only is it the great people he surrounds himself with that are key, but also the way he impacts on those around him.

What is it like to be in Rick's orbit? How does this people-centric person inspire others? Unsurprisingly, it is never hard to get his colleagues to open up. They are endlessly invigorated by his infectious energy.

Here's what a few of them had to say:

> 'Rick is a really smart guy. There are some great salespeople out there. There are some analytical people and some great managers. What is rare is to find that combination of characteristics to that extent in the same person.'

> 'I don't know of anybody else who can work as successfully at a strategic 30,000-foot level, and then take a deep dive into the details and be as proficient at that.'

> 'He can process information; he can draw conclusions from it. He can draw follow-up questions from it. Those characteristics, along with his salesmanship, are a unique combination. Some people are good at the analytical part, but not as good at expressing it.'

> 'He's passionate, courageous, humble, bold, perseverant, optimistic, authentic, infectious, upbeat, self-aware and mentally tough.'

> 'His enthusiasm comes through instantly in his energy and you can feel his passion, along with a great sense of humour.'

Michael Spencer: Founder and CEO, NEX Group (formerly ICAP)

When we compare business to warfare, caveats are required. Nobody dies and the 'enemy' is a law-abiding rival rather than a force of evil. There are, however, many similarities and when

Michael Spencer talks about his journey to the stratosphere, one senses that he could equally have led an army. Like a battleground, Michael's broking business, ICAP, required incredible inspirational leadership.

Michael has never been one to sit still. He was born in British Malaya, where his father, an economist, worked for the colonial government. Michael's childhood was typical of the British expat community. He and his family moved from Malaya to Sudan, and then on to Ethiopia, staying long enough in each place to settle down before being whisked away to start again. His leather suitcase was packed and unpacked regularly in his first eight years, until it was time for him to set off alone to a boys' boarding school in England.

It may be a cliché, but this sort of background fosters resilience and independence. It was a tough environment for a young boy, but Michael flourished, excelling in the sciences. His academic prowess led him to the hallowed halls of Oxford where he read physics and, ironically for a stratospheric leader, thought about going on to study astrophysics.

However, Michael had bigger plans. He knew he wouldn't follow in his father's footsteps. He wasn't going to travel Britain's former empire; he was going to found his own.

Michael decided to start in the City. He moved once again, found himself a desk at a City broker and learned his trade. He also learned that he did not like the way the business worked. The 'pea-soupers' of Victorian London had been exchanged for a thick fog of complacency in the City. He saw that many firms were playing petty politics instead of driving forward. Fierce competition between individuals negated the benefits of teamwork and impacted adversely on profit.

He had vision and he invested in nurturing that vision, as well as his own start-up. In 1986, he founded ICAP with just three other brokers and £50,000 of his own capital. Michael admits that he wasn't providing anything new. As someone who had considered an astrophysics degree, he says that it wasn't rocket science. There were twenty-three other firms in London at the time doing what he did, but they didn't have the battle plan. They didn't have Michael.

Machiavelli advised leaders to make mistakes of ambition, not sloth (Reader's Literary Classics, 2021), and Michael was certainly ambitious. He played right up at the net, always pushing forward, cutting off angles and looking opponents in the eye. This enabled him to develop real differentiators. Other brokers paid their staff salaries that grew over time; ICAP brokers were paid a percentage of the commission they generated. Other brokers were largely paper based and worked off old monitors; ICAP brokers were the first in the City to use live screens. This put them in pole position to take advantage of the Big Bang.

The financial world was changing, the global economy was in flux and the workplace was evolving. It was a time that required vision and bravery. General Spencer was always ready to risk his entire stake on his next move. He knew that the advent of the euro would be a deciding factor for ICAP, so he started to form a multinational team and encouraged a Eurocentric business. Like an intrepid explorer, he had conquered new lands before they were even on the map.

ICAP was on a roll. Michael kept building his team, bringing in captains of industry to take the company into new innovative directions. There was a sense of this being something bigger than boutique and it was time to see how far it could go.

Enter the millennium and ICAP was going from strength to strength. The firm went public in 1998 with the reverse takeover of

Exco, a much larger competitor that was on the brink of collapse. The market cap of ICAP was a modest £40 million at the end of the first day of trading. A merger with listed Garban followed a year later, creating the largest inter-dealer broker globally. Within two years, ICAP had gone from being a powerful boutique to a behemoth. The share price rocketed.

By the middle of the millennium's first decade, Michael was the head of a broking firm with 5,000 employees and 60 offices worldwide. With a huge global footprint, ICAP had undeniably crushed the competition. Most of the firms that had been jockeying for position in the City when ICAP was founded had now disappeared or merged.

A keen philanthropist, Spencer also founded the ICAP Charity Day in 1993, an annual event in which royalty and celebrities man the trading desks at ICAP and the broking firm donates the day's revenue to charities. The event has raised over $150 million and backed 2,200 charitable projects.

In 2006, the ICAP share price had risen to the point that the company joined the FTSE 100 Index. There are few FTSE companies where the founder is also the CEO, but when ICAP was listed in 2006, Michael remained at the helm. What is it that makes Michael different? He believes his science degree gave him the analytical advantage over the people he worked alongside in his early broking career. His peers believe it is his formidable nature and his ability to execute precise strategy.

Speaking to Michael, one notices just how heavily his words are littered with military metaphor. He sees his business strategy as a battle plan; the markets are his theatres of war; and he is the general who will lead his troops to victory. Here is a man who came from the outer reaches of the British Empire in its twilight and built his own empire from the ground up.

What sets Michael apart is his ability to think like the great leaders he reads about: Napoleon, Nelson, Eisenhower and Churchill (with whom he shares the name Spencer). He has been described by some as ruthless. He says you have to be ready to disrupt what you have done in the past to see what you can achieve in the future. Tough talk that is always backed up by action.

In December 2016, Michael sold ICAP's voice-broking business to Tullett Prebon. He rebranded the electronic markets and post-trade services side of the former ICAP to NEX Group, which was subsequently acquired by CME Group in 2018.

Michael may have realised his long-held dream of building an empire, but he has no intention of easing up. Spencer was granted peerage by UK Prime Minister Boris Johnson, and now sits in the House of Lords. His focus is still on tomorrow and the next campaign. Stratospheric leaders need to be relentless in their pursuit of success and Michael Spencer is nothing if not relentless.

Lee Olesky: Founder, Chairman and CEO, Tradeweb

Stratospheric leaders, by definition, live on the boundaries. They live every second of their lives to the full. That kind of pace guarantees peaks and troughs – luck and disaster, success and survival are all familiar bedfellows.

What may be most extraordinary about stratospheric leaders is their ability to find a balance between the different spheres of their lives. Somehow, they find time to nourish work, family, passions and sports, despite commanding billion-dollar enterprises. Lee Olesky is the living embodiment of this balance.

Despite having led Tradeweb from start-up to a multibillion-dollar business, Lee is a man who personifies balance. His focus is multidimensional, and he has the extraordinary ability to home in on any particular area at the right time and give it complete focus.

Balance begins at home and family is Lee's nucleus. He grew up in New Jersey in the 1970s, at a time when kids played street hockey, rode their bikes and stayed outside until they were called in for dinner. It was a time when the American dream felt realisable and possibilities were endless. Lee talks about how lucky he was to live in an environment where family came together for meals, where neighbours talked over fences and kids felt safe and supported. This confluence of serendipitous influences gave him the most stable of backgrounds and he has replicated that in his adult life. His parents are still his rock, along with his own wife and kids. Family remains his anchor, his insulation and his guiding force.

Leadership has been omnipresent for Lee. He was voted captain of his school tennis team, not because he was the best player, but because his teammates saw that he was the most supportive. He was trustworthy, confident and worked hard to lift his teammates up.

Hall of Famer Peyton Manning brilliantly observed, 'The most valuable player is the one that makes the most players valuable' (Canal, 2016). That has been Lee's superpower. He led that way at school, in the early days of Tradeweb, and still leads in exactly the same way now.

At school, Lee was smart, conscientious and a genuine all-rounder. He loved to read about the great leaders of history, from senators to warriors. He followed his passion and studied history at Tulane University. He thrived, thanks to a combination of his appetite for learning, his remarkable work ethic and the inspiration he found from his tutors.

As a successful graduate, like so many of his peers, he fell into a career in law. Having qualified, he spent two years in M&As – long enough for him to understand that this was not the right path for him to follow. For some, this would present a dilemma; a fear that time had been wasted and opportunities lost. Not for Lee. He is a person who knows the value of hard work and that nothing is ever given to him on a plate. He often speaks of hard work being the minimum requirement. Whatever came next, hard work and passion would take him wherever he wanted to go.

Lee pivoted and found a role at First Boston bank. Personable and intelligent, he managed risk and made good decisions. By the time First Boston became Credit Suisse, Lee held a senior leadership role.

As chief operating officer (COO) of the bank's fixed-income business, Lee demonstrated a quality that is common across the stratosphere. He stepped away from the helter-skelter of the trading floor and the day-to-day challenges of the business to find time to think.

When you meet Lee, it is striking how interesting and how interested he is. This is a man who is a voracious learner, reading five to six papers every day; a man who takes time to reflect, to plan; a man who can take a blueprint from his learning. He did what he was great at: quietly analysing where the system could work better. What Lee saw was a trading floor where people were so focused on winning the game in the short term, they were overlooking failings within the system. Human errors abounded and these were errors that only a computer system could catch.

In 1996, Lee founded Tradeweb. It was the simplest of ideas: an online treasury bond market that made it possible for a trader to find prices without making a myriad of phone calls. That was it. Just like Lee himself, the idea was straightforward, credible, reliable and intelligent, and as with so many of our other CEOs, it came at exactly the right moment. The internet was transitioning from a quirky hangout for computer scientists into a mainstream service that was about to transform the world.

With consortium backing from banks such as Goldman Sachs, Lehman Brothers and Credit Suisse, Tradeweb set out to rival its own backers. This may sound strange, but for its backers, it was the ultimate hedge – if it didn't work, they could continue to make profits as normal; if it did, they would have a stake in the future game. Lee's easy nature, personal relationships, obvious intellect and previous credentials made him a good bet.

Like so many great businesses based on technology, Tradeweb was disintermediating the market. It became the middleman, allowing buyers and sellers to trade instantly. Others had the same idea, but Lee moved fast and within three years, he had eleven major banks using his platform.

Tradeweb is a thriving, progressive environment at the cutting edge of real-time markets where the energy is palpable. The most important question at Tradeweb is: 'What's next?' Every employee knows that Lee will give them a platform on which to grow. It's a different league to the school team, but everyone feels supported to win.

One of Lee's zones of genius is his ability to see a way to have the most impact in any situation. He talks about 'lazy hard work', by which he means finding the optimal way to make the most of the short time you have. Take out the noise and interference and find the most hyper-efficient route from position A to position B. It comes as no surprise that Lee's career arc took the same direct trajectory.

Tradeweb went from a start-up in 1996 to an initial public offering (IPO) of $12 billion in 2019 – one of the most successful IPOs of that year. That moment was a huge inflexion point for Lee. He could have stopped there, but he doesn't stop – for Lee, there is no end point. In 1999, he had already begun working on another start-up, focusing on the inter-dealer market, allowing banks to trade with other banks. Meet BrokerTec. Goldman Sachs allowed Lee to nurture this baby to the point where ICAP bought it out just three years after its inception – for $240 million.

Under Lee's vision, Tradeweb has grown from an embryonic pipe dream into a sprawling giant. You will see the footprint of the company everywhere in the electronic market: in US corporate bonds; in European exchange-traded funds; in the Chinese bond market. If you want a practical definition of 'stratospheric', try this: in a single day of trading, more money passes through Tradeweb's systems than through the entire US stock market.

Yet Lee continues to strike a balance. He takes time every day to read, staying abreast of all that is happening in the markets and in the world, while studying history books because he is a thoughtful, cerebral person who loves to stretch his mind. He exercises daily, making time for it. He knows (like so many of the CEOs I work with) that the physical and mental benefits of exercise affect stamina and focus. He prioritises and his time is highly boundaried.

It is this self-awareness that allows Lee to remain at the top. He knows what he needs in his life to maintain his energy and his passions, and his habits pay him back. He feeds off the energy he reaps from balancing his passions. That is why, even at the peak, Lee continues to look to the next summit.

Lee retired as CEO of Tradeweb in December 2022 and announced his retirement as Chairman of the Board in May 2023. His pioneering efforts in electronic trading have revolutionised the markets, leaving a lasting legacy. Now he is embarking on the next chapter of his life, and, I imagine, enjoying quality time with his family and pursuing his personal passions. I wish him the very best.

Henry Fernandez:
Founder, Chairman and CEO, MSCI Inc

Henry is a leader with a difference. Working at MSCI, he didn't set his sights on making a decent bonus or pushing for his next promotion – he dreamt of more. He identified a niche, an unmined area of capital, and while his contemporaries fought their way up the existing ladder, he created his own.

Nearly three decades ago, Henry formed, nurtured, sharpened and piloted MSCI, and under his guidance, it flourished. Since spinning out from Morgan Stanley in 2007, MSCI's share price has risen by 28X and some $15 trillion of investor assets are now benchmarked against its indices.

You would be forgiven for making some assumptions about Henry: that he came from a moneyed family; that he has finance in his genes; that he had been nurtured for this destiny; that he looks and sounds like the stereotype of an alpha male leader. Those would all be fair guesses, but the real Henry is much more interesting. He wasn't born in the US; nor did he have the benefit of a banking background. His is an extraordinary, inspiring self-made success story.

Henry is Nicaraguan. His family were close, but life was tough. Henry balanced his studies with caring for his older brother, Armando, who suffered from severe cerebral palsy. He describes his brother as his 'guiding light'. His father was in the military and often away from home, and Henry was the man of the house when he was absent. He bore the weight of responsibility, feeling he needed to live his life for himself and Armando.

He was an introverted boy who disliked sports and had few material possessions of his own. From his father, he inherited a love of books, and he read voraciously about anything, but mostly focusing on history and great leaders. He may not have excelled on track or field, but he tested the limits of his confidence by riding motocross bikes where time and money allowed.

Henry is the first to admit that he had a stroke of luck. The ruling family in Nicaragua were searching for talented people to join the government and the military, and his father managed to arrange an introduction. Henry didn't need to be asked twice. His potential was spotted immediately and he was offered funding for college, paving the way for a future career in public service.

He was awarded a scholarship to Georgetown and the Nicaraguan president appointed him to be a diplomat in the country's Nicaraguan embassy in Washington. Yes, while the rest of us might have been working behind a bar in the evenings to fund our undergraduate lives, Henry was representing his country and learning the skills of diplomacy and negotiation. He was being primed for his return to Nicaragua and he dreamt of the changes that he could make in the homeland he loved.

While Henry was in Washington, a Marxist revolution spread through Nicaragua. The ruling elite were swept away, and along with them went Henry's predetermined future. At the time, Henry's father was visiting him in Washington from Nicaragua for a few days to solicit military and economic support from the US Government for the existing regime. Henry begged him to remain in the United States, safe from the political machinations back home, since the fall of the government was imminent and his life would be in great danger. His father's determination to do what he considered his duty and return, despite the real risk to his life, made a deep and long-lasting impact on his son.

Henry decided to reach for different stars. He wanted to become a citizen of the world and explore new places and find new ideas. To do so, he initially focused on two challenges: to complete his degree and to win US citizenship to enable him to fulfil his potential. He achieved both, spending his summers travelling and learning, developing a truly global perspective on life. He enrolled at Stanford, where he found an environment that encouraged the realisation of possibility. Surrounded by creativity and imagination, his can-do spirit thrived. He breathed rarefied air and wanted more.

Henry is not the only person to have moved countries, to have pushed himself through education, to have created wealth from a standing start. There is more to him than his story. There is as much for us to learn from his authenticity as from his tenacity.

A former boss once suggested Henry should take elocution lessons. He refused. Not only was he proud of his Latin roots, but he had a greater purpose. This is a man who set out to change the world, not his accent. He is described by his employees as honest, fearless, terrific, bold, visionary and tenacious – not what you might imagine from a natural introvert who is also small in stature. He is relentless in asking, 'What's next?', always inquisitive, always raising the bar.

Henry loves to work, regardless of the hour or the day, but he defines work a little differently to most. He dedicates time to daydreaming, he reads voraciously, he cares passionately about his legacy and never letting an opportunity fester. He has created a role that he loves. Sending an email on a Sunday doesn't feel like an imposition, more the enjoyment of a hobby.

In my experience, Henry exudes a rare warmth that envelops you the moment you engage in conversation. His gift of storytelling, coupled with his boundless generosity of spirit, meant I left our conversations feeling not only uplifted, energised and inspired, but truly transformed. Henry's infectious passion for life and visionary nature have made him a formidable leader in the industry.

You will read much more about Henry, an inspirational introvert who has created his own route to – and place within – the stratosphere, later in this book.

Chris Willcox: Executive Officer and Head of Wholesale, Nomura

Chris Willcox's career affords us a unique viewpoint of – and additional context around – our fintech founders. He has, at different stages, been a customer, a user, a counterparty stakeholder, a board member and a partner in Tradeweb, MarketAxess, ICAP, MSCI and IHS Markit. His inclusion in this book is primarily because he is not only an incredibly successful and accomplished leader in his own right, but one of the most intentional people you could meet. He has navigated his life and career by creating his own compass – a set of leadership lessons that guide his mindset, decision making and behaviours every day.

In his own journey, Chris could never be accused of taking the easy route. He is an adventurer at heart. He loves complexity and to be tested, whether that be in his personal passions or at work. He is a man who has learned to find comfort in discomfort.

As a child, Chris had the usual dreams that youngsters have of becoming a firefighter or joining the Navy. Perhaps this latter dream was influenced by his father, a marine engineer. Being an expat child with parents whose jobs kept them overseas, Chris spent his childhood in a UK boarding school – a place where he learned resilience, fortitude and self-reliance.

At school, he found he was drawn to academic life. When it came time to leave, his parents would have loved for him to follow the Oxbridge route, but London, in the form of University College London and LSE, called to Chris. He thrived, completing not only his bachelor's, but his master's degree. He considered a PhD, but he saw that all the top-notch academics of his generation were going to the US, which was too expensive compared to the UK, where he benefited from an Economic and Social Research Council scholarship. Others among his peers were assuming positions in the merchant banks of London, but those jobs were still heavily dependent on family connections that Chris's background didn't come with. Instead, Chris hit the trading floor, thinking he could save enough money to return to academia later.

His was only the second intake of graduates in London into Citibank. Like many of our other CEOs, Chris was on the floor in the infancy of electronic trading. A time when desk phones were always buzzing, deals were being struck and rules were made to be broken. The fast-paced lifestyle meant that Chris knew he 'would only have a half-life of a few years'. People over forty were almost unheard of on a dealing floor.

Once you get sucked in, you are in, and Chris was in for two decades. These were formative times for him. Having had the early experience of self-reliance at boarding school from the age of seven, he had an independent nature, which was compounded by an environment that was pressurised, scrutinised and exposed. It wasn't a place where there was time for mentoring or coaching. Chris learned to double-down on his resilient, individualistic nature; he was adept at the work and he climbed the ladder accordingly.

Chris is driven, dedicated and determined, but like so many of the CEOs I work with, he talks about luck. These leaders know that there is some degree of serendipity to their stellar rise. Chris is always humble. He knows that there are many people out there who have worked as hard as he did but may not have had the breaks.

After fifteen years at Citibank, and at the time Asia-Pacific head of global rates, currencies and commodities, Chris joined JP Morgan.

His compass led him on an extraordinary journey – moving from the sell side to the buy side, from the UK to the US where he would ultimately become CEO of JP Morgan Asset Management. Chris was operating in a global environment with exceptional reach, and he had few industry peers with a broader portfolio of assets. It was an environment where he could thrive. In each area of the business, his presence was felt, and he built exciting, values-driven cultures where colleagues could succeed. His principled approach meant that people felt appreciated.

Chris created a legacy at JP Morgan. He instilled direction and innovation. He was always looking to do things differently and better; to break and remake a model for success. Chris shared the compass that drove him with his teams, providing everyone with a benchmark and a framework for success.

Never one to sit still for long, Chris has taken on the challenge of global leadership as the first non-Japanese person to be appointed executive officer of Nomura Holdings. As with any role, he knows it will come with challenges, but that is Chris's natural environment. In troubled waters, Chris always has a calm head. For him, the complexity of the problem comes with the possibility of great intellectual reward.

Like a moth to a flame, Chris is drawn to anything that tests his limits – both professionally and personally. He has sailed across the Atlantic, trekked in the Himalayas and dived at some of the world's most dangerous wrecks. I am sure there will be many more adventures.

Chris is serious, thoughtful and cerebral, with bucketloads of integrity. He is a man who is open to change. He draws people in and wants them to become superstars. He will go above and beyond to deliver, not only for the investors and the board, but also for the team.

He is fascinating to watch, because even though he is what we would classically term an introvert, he is a powerful figure in the public arena. He is a thoughtful leader whose decisive style and clarity of communication create loyalty and followership. His storytelling captivates and he is engaging, charismatic and memorable, a powerhouse of the town hall. His people know that he will stand shoulder to shoulder with them and hold himself accountable for the wins and losses of the team. The buck always stops with him.

Chris does have a compass that guides him. This is his way marker for excellence and it has created a track record of success, which he has embedded in each of the teams he has led. His compass has become a foundation for many, and in this book, he has allowed me to share aspects of it with you.

PART ONE

THE LESSONS

ONE

An Audacious Vision

> 'My whole management style is to set audacious goals and work really hard to reach them. You need to have goals that are inspirational and believe in them. You have to dream where you are going.'

Lance Uggla

It's quite something to be in a plane on a clear day, looking down at the view below. At altitude, the perspective can be extraordinary. We see huge sweeps of land and sea; we understand the impact of mountains, lakes and rivers on the environment around them.

When we are up in the sky, thinking about the big picture can be relatively easy. What is infinitely harder is benefiting from that wider view before we take flight, because we live in a world of noise and information overload, where clarity and perspective can be challenging.

A factor uniting every one of our stratospheric leaders is the desire to reinvent part of the universe or even set out to discover or create some new places. They have a dream. They can see the evolution of technologies and markets. They can visualise, build, connect opportunities and create new value, which most people don't even realise could be possible or needed until they have it.

Despite commencing their careers within established global banks, the leaders featured in this book consistently embody an entrepreneurial spirit – in fact, one was described by a former bank colleague as having been an 'entrepreneur in residence'. This is a quality they might not have initially acknowledged within themselves, but it was certainly evident to those around them.

When I started writing this book, I initially described the goals of these CEOs as 'moon-shot' in a bid to convey the magnitude of their aspiration. However, upon reflection, I realised that aiming for the moon simply isn't bold enough. The moon, after all, has already had humans land, with flags planted to prove it. The goals of these leaders are more stratospheric – penetration into rarefied atmospheres – and their vision is their navigation tool.

Stratospheric leaders are those building extraordinary companies. They believe in the business of problems looking for solutions, even those problems that are not yet widely acknowledged or perceived to exist.

Each of these leaders has a key unifying superpower – audacious vision and ambition – and that, combined with their exceptional skills in management, communication and leadership, has created multibillion-dollar enterprises that have transformed financial markets. Unlocking creativity, seeing opportunities and connecting components of the market are all skills that can be developed, intentionally cultivated and refined. The impossible can be made possible.

When we think about entrepreneurship or leadership, we may assume it is something that happens to us as we rise the corporate ladder or as opportunities are afforded to us. Being invited behind the curtain and spending hundreds of hours in conversation with stratospheric leaders, seeing what they do and how they do it, I have learned a massive amount. The key learning has been that their success, impact and influence are not by chance; they're by design, carefully cultivated, crafted and curated.

When we look at world-class athletes or entertainers, we recognise they bring discipline, commitment, unwavering focus and determination – a high-performance winning mindset as well as physical excellence – to what they do. I consider stratospheric leaders to be corporate athletes. They have intense ambition, a confidence and a spark within them that is electric. Whether consciously or subconsciously, they foster that ambition, training it and honing it with a rigorous focus and commitment. The physical element is the hours, travel, stress running constantly throughout their lives. Their success is the product of deliberate intent and a relentless pursuit of their objectives.

Here, the stratospheric CEOs share some of their strategies for nurturing their audacious ambition.

Enabling daydreaming

If you set out to run a marathon, you become intentional about the way you use the muscles in your body. If you set out to become a world-class violinist, you become intentional about the way you move your hands and interpret the music. When one thinks about leadership in the corporate or financial arena, however, one rarely thinks of intentional ambition. Success is usually considered to come as a result of serendipity, the markets, the company, but world-class business leaders at their core are just like athletes and musicians. They have unwavering ambition, relentless and rigorous mindsets, and they persevere.

A core element that the stratospheric leaders profiled in this book share is the intention with which they approach their markets, business and products. They each describe it somewhat differently, but their intention can be distilled into a word rarely used to describe successful individuals – they daydream.

The word may have childish connotations, but ultimately, daydreaming is a state of calm existence that enables your conscious (or subconscious) to imagine and visualise and not be consumed by the noises of routine task objectives. Henry Fernandez shared that he makes time to daydream. This has been a powerful enabler for him, allowing his inspiration to come naturally verses recycling old ideas. He propels himself into the future, dreams where he is going, and then focuses on the *how* – moving his ideas into effective execution (the execution piece is critical and will be discussed further in Chapter Three). This is something few do.

Whether we describe daydreaming as intellectual curiosity, meditation or reflective time, it is a core part of the leaders featured in this book and something they foster and cultivate. In their periods of daydreaming, which can be either solitary or interactive, they are constantly soliciting insight and data (through their internal thoughts or their external conversations and interactions) to feed into reshaping tomorrow.

Here are some examples of questions they ask themselves while daydreaming:

- 'What am I/are we going to do to change the world?'

- 'What does a higher goal look and feel like?'

- 'What risks will I take?'

- 'What sacrifices will I endure?'

- 'What stamina will I need?'

- 'What may be possible in a decade or two?'

They are continually pushing and prodding themselves to be thinking in stratospheric directions. Their curiosity, combined with deep ambition and desire, has proven to be a winning formula.

Connecting, collecting and learning

For Michael Spencer, creativity begins by him taking the long view. ICAP was not necessarily doing anything radical or inventive, but his vision was always to look forward, rethink and innovate execution to do things differently and better. Part of this involved regularly questioning himself and his leadership team to identify trends:

> 'How do you think this business is going to look in five or ten years? Will it look the same? If it's not looking the same, what does it look like? More people? Fewer people? More human intervention? Less human intervention? More global? Less global? What are the changes you think will happen?'

For Henry Fernandez, creativity and ingenuity begin forensically. A thirst for knowledge was present in his childhood, and he has modified and refined it through his leadership journey, recognising its intrinsic value. He sets aside time to learn about success and leadership. He reads articles; not ones that provide the answers, but those that provoke his thinking. He studies history to understand cycles – you can get a lot right in the wrong cycle and win little to nothing in a good one.

Henry also reads autobiographies of people who have endured and achieved enormous personal, business or societal transformation, making the impossible happen. He studies pioneers like Albert Einstein who have changed the course of history, John Maynard Keynes who transformed economics and Alexander the Great, one of history's finest military minds.

Henry looks at the past – the triumphs, the attitudes and the mindsets these individuals brought to their endeavours. What did each one do every day? Did they wake up and make their own decisions or did they have advisors? Who was in their trusted circle? What were their motivations? He reflects, he learns and he collects valuable data points and parameters, which feed into how he establishes his vision to change the investment world. Like all the CEOs in the book, he studies the mistakes great people made as well as their successes, recognising the importance of and the learning that can be gleaned from failure. He sees the world as his classroom:

> 'I learn a great deal from people everywhere. From people in the elevator to political leaders and public CEOs. It's just a question of being humble and being open to learning in totally unexpected places, as opposed to a structured program.'

Being intellectually curious has given Henry the gift of understanding human nature. As he shared with his children, 'If you do not understand human nature, you are going to make a lot of mistakes in life.'

The modern world finds humankind in a state of busyness, so finding time to think can be difficult. It requires discipline to make time for reflection and creative thought, along with recognition that creativity can happen in the most unexpected places. You may be sitting at a conference, watching a movie, at a cocktail party or in the shower when a thought is triggered.

Take advantage of these opportune times and elaborate on that thought. Creativity doesn't follow rules for when it appears, but it does need space to emerge. If you don't capitalise on it, eventually somebody else will.

Nature or nurture? The CEOs in this book are always learning from individuals past and present, using every opportunity as a teaching moment to frame their thinking. It is a skill they have nurtured. They have cultivated and refined it, knowing the yield it brings. The great news is that you can do the same.

Intentional innovation

For Michael, the changes he made with ICAP can all look obvious in retrospect, whether they were triggered by the advent of the euro, the electronification of the markets or the globalisation of banking. His questioning and long-term play, however, meant Michael made decisions that future-proofed his business, while many of his competitors continued to show up and do what they did yesterday.

Lance Uggla also believes in dreaming big and visualising the future to enable intentional innovation. He says, 'You've got to dream where you're going. If you dream you're going to go up three steps, you'll get up three steps, but why not dream you're going to go to the top?' His relentlessness, boundless energy and charisma have been core characteristics in delivering high-margin businesses and building organic and inorganic capabilities at scale.

For Lance, Markit's intentional innovation was to provide transparency to previously opaque markets, offering better quality pricing data to allow them to function more efficiently for all participants. Like all the CEOs in the book, he had a background in the industry where he was innovating. He knew the landscape, had the market knowledge and understood how it needed to change.

He saw the transparency that the equity markets had gone through in the 1990s and the limitation of pricing knowledge in the credit market. Recognising the value that could be created in the credit markets and beyond with greater transparency, he had the idea, the vision and the conviction to execute.

Audacious and ambitious goals

Manifest destiny theory (O'Sullivan, 1845) explores the idea that every person can make a difference in the world by effecting change. Henry buys into this. He doesn't just have lofty dreams, he believes that the size and scope of his dreams give him an advantage over those who set more easily realisable goals. Mediocre goals create mediocre outcomes. At MSCI, his vision is one of changing the investment industry for the better; specifically, Henry wants to create a better allocation of capital in the world.

Lance believes in setting big hairy audacious goals (BHAGs) (Collins, Porras, 1994) or wildly inspiring goals (WIGs) (Covey, 2015). He asks everybody from his team to share a BHAG or WIG, creating goals he believes in and can mathematically map on to paper.

He shared with me his thousand-dollar share-price goal and the roadmap of what his teams would have to do in terms of acquisitions, share buy-backs, capital allocation and growth to be able to achieve that price. In ten years, it was mathematically possible.

Being audacious involves having confidence in your ambitions and changing the questions and the parameters of your thinking. Elevate the expectations of yourself and your leadership team, and you will change the magnitude of the outcome and the mindset of your people.

Billion-dollar companies are built from solving challenges that may not be recognised yet or are seen to be impossible or insurmountable. When you find your goal, rarely will it start big, but it does need to start somewhere. The key questions to ask then are, 'Is my goal scalable? How can I size my target market? How will I measure success?' From a go-to-market perspective, the best leaders are constantly asking, 'How big could or should this goal be?'

The leaders in this book are all domicile and industry experts who have ultimately used their knowledge and experience to make change across markets that no one else saw or acted on. They do their research and get granular about their business goals.

Rick McVey speaks of this being essential before diving straight in. Is there client validation? How clear are you on the size of your market? Preparation is key to ensure your gut instinct is correct. Ultimately, you will need those data points to seek funding and convince investors to invest in the company and its audacious goal. They're the validation points you can use to inspire those you want to motivate and influence your ability to hire A+ players to be a part of the mission to achieve the goal.

Communicating audacity – internally and externally

Once you have your audacious goal, you now need to take something ethereal and articulate it in a compelling and tangible way to make it real for people. No rudder means no direction. How will your audacious goal make things better? Remember that if you can't clearly and consistently link your goal to a healthy financial performance, unless you're lucky, you'll be waiting to be surprised, likely in a bad way!

What stood out for me in our conversations wasn't just the words the stratospheric CEOs used to describe their goals, but *how* they described the goal, the vision, the dream. Their energy, passion and enthusiasm were infectious and palpable. Their state of being created a contagion in their goal that others wanted to be part of. The way in which they communicated it meant it evolved and became a 'live' organism within the company and leadership team.

Often leaders focus on the *what*, ie the words they share, when it is the *how* that moves people to action. The stratospheric CEOs' unwavering and unshakable belief, along with the way they expressed it, was a key component in getting their people on board to realise their audacious goals, instilling confidence in them.

If you have clearly articulated your audacious goals, you will hear your vision repeated by your teams and your clients, on panels, on social media and in internal meetings. Listening in, without too much filtering or cherry picking (we all have a confirmation bias), on how others have interpreted your vision will provide you with valuable feedback, offering insights where small course corrections are needed. The course corrections are rarely 180 degrees, more 5-degree shifts to the left or right. Refinements should be constant and gradual, as turning hard left or hard right can be tough and people adapt slowly.

The most important piece of advice here is to leverage your strategic sense as a leader. Use all five senses to glean intelligence. Insight and data are all around you, if you choose to be present and activate the power of your senses.

Be discerning about which voices you listen to

Audacious goals are about taking people to places where they do not yet know they need to go. When you are doing things others haven't, there will be many voices offering their opinions, and a lesson the stratospheric leaders learned early on in their entrepreneurial journey is not every voice counts.

There will be the champions and supporters. There will also be naysayers, cynics, sceptics and doubters who can't or don't want to believe you can achieve your ambitious goals. Some will be jealous that you had the idea first and the courage of conviction; others won't be able to see the future through the same lens as you because their view is too narrow or short term. Maybe they are just resistant because most people are fundamentally uncomfortable with change and embracing the unknown.

How do you manage the voices? Rick shares that one of the keys to his career success has been the importance of listening to gather information.

> 'At every meeting, you can learn something, no matter who you are sitting down with, if you listen more than you talk and you ask the right questions. You will never have 100% certainty on the tough decisions, but at some point, you get to a level of confidence that you are all green to go, and you are not going to let the doubters stop you.'

Lee Olesky emphasises that not everything you hear will be easy to take, saying, 'It's important to listen to the criticism, but not to take it personally.'

As an entrepreneur entering new territories, you should never be surprised if you hit resistance. In fact, you should expect it; it's simply a matter of figuring out how you are going to work around it. Rick's strategy is to be persistent and tenacious and overwhelm the doubters with facts. Recognise what they pay attention to. What do they ultimately care about?

Importantly, it is about leveraging the opinions of believers. Although Rick's objective is not to win over the pessimists, continuing to move forward in the face of doubt creates its own momentum and can potentially over time convert the naysayers.

One method of conversion is to demonstrate why what you are doing is good for the naysayers; another is to leverage stakeholders who can maximise the impact. For example, Rick recognised that for MarketAxess, the key was getting the investment management clients to buy into the idea, because if they started changing their behaviour, the banks would pay attention.

Stratospheric leaders are never surprised when they hit resistance. It's not a blocker, simply an obstacle to work around. They recognise early on the importance of focusing on the voices and feedback that matter and giving limited attention to the rest.

Sounds simple, yet it can be incredibly hard not to get distracted by the clamour. It's a super skill each stratospheric CEO has cultivated, figuring out which voices to respect. Everyone can have a voice, but not everyone has a vote. Stratospheric CEOs look at where the best use of their time is and understand that leveraging 50.01% of the opinions (and votes) is what matters.

Henry shared:

> 'When I was twenty years old, my father, who was a military leader, took me to lunch with a renowned figure in Latin America. He had run a country and his father had also run a country.
>
> 'I asked him, "General, tell me, what is it that your father had that made him who he was?"
>
> 'He paused, thought about it a little bit, and then said, "My father had the ability to see the future and to work in the present to achieve the future." I never forgot what he said, because I was mesmerised by it. I knew then that

was the magic. The ability to see the future and work in the present to achieve it. There's nothing else in the world that is better than that.'

Summary

What unites the leaders profiled in this book is that in each case, their business success started with one powerful, landscape-altering idea. They created the audacious goal, the vision, the strategy, communicated it, tracked it and changed it when required.

Stratospheric CEOs are long-term dreamers with a *big* ambition and a powerful vision for transformation. They're unique in their ability to recognise an unmet scalable need that people don't even know they're missing and connect opportunities, coupled with getting people behind their vision. Vision without followership is delusion. Followership based on reality (not cultism) is rare, but common across all our leaders.

Most importantly, our stratospheric CEOs have the audacity, confidence, courage and expansive perspective to dream and believe. Without the singularity of their vision, their unswerving focus, they'd be going nowhere. They make the impossible possible.

As one of their colleagues shared, 'Never bet against these CEOs.'

TWO

Risk Is Possibility

'A lot of people misinterpret risk taking.'

Henry Fernandez

Alex Honnold is the climber who scaled Freerider on El Capitan without ropes (Synnott, 2019). It was, according to the climbing community, impossible.

Alex isn't reckless, though. He asked questions, he listened and he assessed the risks involved. He was driven by an aspiration, and he was willing to stake his life on achieving it. Luckily, the boardroom is not a place where you are risking your life (although at times it can feel like that), but sometimes, you do have to scale metaphorical cliffs without the comfort of ropes to hold you on the wall.

Like Alex Honnold, what marks out the CEOs profiled in this book is that potential risk isn't something that stops them, because it is calculated and considered. They have faith and are optimistic that they will figure things out and find a way to achieve their goal. What others deem to be impossible is, in their opinion, possible.

When you have the stratospheric goal, how do you know whether you can stomach the risk involved? It is easy to talk about transformation and innovation, but then you have to step into the unknown. How do you know at the outset what your appetite for risk *really* is? What price are you willing to pay? How much risk are you willing to take? What sacrifices are you prepared to make?

The climb to the stratosphere will involve icy stretches, crevices to circumvent, huge rocks to negotiate, and periods of fear and loneliness. It's part of the journey in achieving the audacious goals. Risk comes with the territory, so what do you need to be thinking about?

Every risk must be calculated

Stratospheric leaders dare to take great risks, but not at any cost or on impulse. Their risk approach is measured and well thought out. They study to understand the stakes involved and to gain knowledge, enabling them to evaluate the value creation versus the value destruction if the risk doesn't pay off.

Henry Fernandez says:

> 'If you're not calculating, you are basically betting, which are two different things. Risk taking is examining the situation, analysing the pros and cons, truly understanding the downsides and coming up with a view that you have an 80%–90% probability of winning, or a 10% probability of losing.'

Perspective is everything. Henry believes the most well-calculated risks pay off, as long as you follow the process.

Lance Uggla's leadership team speaks of his risk-adjusted mentality. He is always quantifying the downside versus the upside of each opportunity, seeking to understand all the outcomes. Risk taking is calculated, not reckless.

Henry believes that many people misinterpret risk taking, saying, 'It's only a small percentage of the time that it won't pay off and the risk will go against you. Many people are risk averse even if they know they have an 80% probability of winning.'

Although the downsides are often not major, most people don't want to pay the price, leading to inaction. They are not willing to lose. What if they make the move, take the decision and it doesn't work out? The anxiety is rarely about losing money or the job. The fear is underpinned by losing face with themselves – they took a bet and it didn't work out, so they compare themselves to others or personalise the outcome. Many lose confidence when this happens, influencing how they approach future opportunities.

Stratospheric leaders are comfortable with taking risk. Lance believes this is where the money is made and where innovations happen. Most people, however, are not natural risk takers. Lance surrounds himself with people who are similar to him and, more importantly, people who can execute and/or balance the risk. Risk is taken by having history and relationships with people, which is one of the areas where Lance is a true maestro.

In today's dynamic world, the unknowns will invariably outweigh the knowns, which means making decisions and taking risks with incomplete data. As Jenny Just, my friend and Co-Founder and Manager Partner at Peak6 Investments, says: 'Becoming less risk averse doesn't mean taking on bigger risk; it means taking on a larger quantity of risks (with an s) and taking them on sooner.' Henry agrees that if by nature you are risk averse, you can transform. You can trick your mind by taking incremental steps to get you more comfortable with risk, finding situations where you can move from risk taking to risk seeking. When you chip away at the uncertainty about taking risks, you start normalising the approach.

Incredible risk takers have got good at it by practice. It's not dissimilar to an athlete who wants to be a championship winner. To become effective at their sport, they constantly have to train their muscles. Risk-taking ability is like a muscle, which strengthens the more you exercise it.

Decisions are rarely black or white

Michael Spencer understands this concept well. He believes the leader who sits on the fence, who prevaricates, is lost. Decision making can be exhausting for some because they tie themselves up in knots, seeking a black-and-white answer. Yes, you can research. Yes, you can seek advice, but you will never have complete certainty, only probability.

Stephen Casper, a former lead director at MarketAxess, describes Rick McVey's method for dealing with probability as opposed to certainty as a 'portfolio approach'. Rather than looking at each decision on its own and in isolation, he instead thinks of it as being part of a portfolio.

This does two things. Firstly, it takes the pressure off every decision needing to be right. So long as more are right than wrong, the overall portfolio is still heading in the right direction. Secondly, it gives you permission to cut out the losses quickly to prevent them from diverting attention and resources that you could be applying to the winners, provided the feedback loop is quick enough for the loss not to be fatal. This means being comfortable with knowing you will sometimes be wrong.

To be a stratospheric entrepreneur, you need to be comfortable beyond most others with uncertainty. This is a function of self-confidence and past success. With the latter, you can draw on the decision-making methodologies you used in past wins and the odds are the methodology, or a derivative of it, will work again.

Stratospheric leaders all have a good sense of risk-adjusted decision making and a great management instinct. They *feel* when something is good. This is critical, but it is hard to teach, because it is cultivated from experience, which takes us back to the concept of exercising your risk-taking muscle.

Not all decisions are created equal. Some will require consideration, consultation and data, while others will not. The decisions that require more input mean speaking to thoughtful people in your network and to the board. This is where diversity of expertise and experience is invaluable, as each person brings a different lens. Stratospheric leaders seek input from different sources to guard against confirmation bias. If you find yourself in an echo chamber, you will simply have your thoughts coming back at you.

The world around us is changing rapidly and as a result, the pace and intensity of decision making has increased. Seemingly, the stakes are bigger, the environment more complex and the number of competing priorities higher. Leaders are required to make hundreds of decisions each week. The key is recognising which are the high-risk decisions and which carry less weight.

The higher the risk quotient, the more stratospheric leaders seek information as they execute the strategy. They are decisive less quickly. If it's a 'bet the farm' decision, they want to make sure they succeed, and even if it's not a home run, they want to ensure the outcome is not a bad one.

For high-stake decisions, stratospheric leaders lean into their curiosity, seeking to learn what they might be missing. In these situations, Lee Olesky asks, 'What corners are we not looking around?'

In some tough or time-pressured situations, you simply have to make a decision with less information than you would like. With a partial instrument panel, the best strategy may be to choose the first good-enough option. A wrong decision subsequently course-corrected is often better than no decision at all.

Mindsets and perceptions

Lance speaks of the hunter versus farmer mindset. He sees entrepreneurs as hunters – those who are willing to take the risk of going out and finding something to eat, otherwise they won't be fed. Whereas the farmer has a nice warm bed every night, a fenced-off property, and they cultivate a piece of land that's creating a consistent yield of plants for food. Although the farm can occasionally get hit by bad weather, it's generally a safe, secure, warm place to live.

Hunters, on the other hand, want to go out and take risks. Occasionally, they will come back with the big game and feed the whole village. Outsized risk brings the potential for outsized rewards. This is what sparks and ignites them.

To the outside world, it can look like a big risk and an outlandish objective to shoot for Mars. People will say no way, others will think you are crazy, but stratospheric leaders can see miles ahead, recognise an unmet need and articulate their vision of how they will make things better, more efficient. With that belief in your vision and trust in your gut instincts, the risks look more like opportunities, and Mars seems closer and more reachable.

All our CEOs share the same stratospheric mindset. They put themselves into the shoes of others to understand what their unmet needs are, to see the opportunities others can't yet see. There are obvious examples among game-changing businesses. When most of us shopped in stores for paperbacks, Amazon was thinking of how the emerging internet could be utilised to become a global bookstore. When we were hailing cabs on the street and standing in the rain as they whistled past us, Uber was looking to connect smart phones, GPS and cars.

Communicating confidence internally and externally

In the economic news, there is a reason why people talk about consumer confidence, investor confidence, business confidence. Boosting confidence is one of the cheapest stimuli that can happen in any economy. If we consider M&A activity, it typically happens when people are optimistic within a company, when there is confidence. The board of directors feels that the organisation should stretch, that they should take risks. Management teams are the same. They believe shareholders will support them in the acquisitions that they make.

These change makers instil confidence across their stakeholders and have confidence in their dreams. Many sink their own personal capital into their business ventures. They back their ideas and invest their heart, soul and relationships to realise the opportunities.

Rick, Lance, Lee and Michael all walked away from successful corporate careers and well-respected positions. It takes courage to leave a role that brings financial security and reputational capital for an environment with many unknown unknowns. Each had the confidence to take calculated risks, following a combination of their convictions, their market knowledge and, ultimately, their capacity to manage and work effectively in an environment of uncertainty.

Nothing spreads confidence like transparency. Where you can, be honest about the risk factors of any business decision and how you are facing them. Be candid with your stakeholders and give them insight into how you are thinking and how you see things panning out. This means showing them you are optimistic and confident about the risk, but not blind to the challenges. Stakeholders value transparency. It fosters trust – the lifeblood of any business.

Lance advises giving more transparency in times of uncertainty by offering investors different scenarios concerning how you see things unfolding. In one of IHS Markit's first board meetings during Covid, he gave the board three different scenarios. Option I: the world starts to recover in the fourth quarter of the year; Option II, the world doesn't recover at all this year; Option III, throughout next year there is a shallow U-shaped recovery. Many CEOs didn't give guidance through this period and as a result, their company's shares sold off and their customers were left feeling uncertain about their future.

Being transparent brings confidence and certainty and avoids people having to second guess. Following Lance's approach, IHS Markit's shares went up, simply as a result of him giving more transparency.

Fear not fear

For some of us, the fear we suffer when we think about risk, stepping into the unknown, can be paralysing, given the likelihood of unforeseen obstacles along the way. Rarely is it a bed of roses or a walk in the park, and as human beings, we typically crave certainty and predictability.

We talk a lot about stress in our modern world. The word 'stress' is interesting in itself – it comes from the Latin *strictus*, meaning 'drawn tight'. This is not necessarily a bad thing – if you have ever tried to shoot an arrow from a bow, you'll know that the only way to do that effectively is by drawing the string tight.

Maybe we need to think about stress differently. The most impactful leaders understand the difference between distress and eustress. Distress is the kind of stress that makes us feel anxious or uncomfortable. Eustress, by contrast, drives us forward. It's the nervous energy that means we can succeed. Healthy pressure will provide the necessary challenge and focus. It is the drawing tight of the bow string that provides the tension we need to hit the bullseye.

In the early twentieth century, psychologists proposed a model that demonstrates a direct correlation between pressure and performance (Yerkes, Dodson, 1908). This relationship is illustrated by an elegant bell curve. Not enough pressure results in underperformance; too much pressure has the same effect. At the top of the curve – at the moment when pressure is perfect and stress becomes eustress – performance is at its peak.

Successful leaders know (consciously or unconsciously) that fear isn't a threat in and of itself. It isn't a distressor but a eustressor: an enabler of momentum. While they may not know all the steps that will get them to their current end goal, they trust themselves, have confidence in their beliefs as well as the self-recognition to course correct as needed.

There isn't an absence of fear for these leaders in pursuit of their goals; their success is more about their relationship with it. They are not afraid of it. They consciously make it a friend, not a foe. If you allow fear to take the driving seat, it will ultimately hinder the heights you can reach.

Lance says, 'Be sure to make mistakes and learn from them. Otherwise, you won't achieve any greatness.' The key is not to be afraid of making those mistakes. Lance will consider the opportunity and say to his leadership team, 'What's the worst outcome? We fail, we lose a bit here, but we're going to gain there.'

Failure isn't failure. Lance sees it as trial and error. He's always challenging, pushing his teams to raise the bar and be better than they were yesterday. Innovation is an iterative process that means always learning, questioning, evolving.

Stratospheric leaders are not afraid to make mistakes on strategy because they know they can learn from them and redirect their investments and their activities to things that will be more productive for them going forward. Rick says, 'You have to be prepared for that part of the journey and be prepared to get kicked in the gut for years.' This means although it isn't easy, it's essential to embrace mistakes and failure.

When you're facing your fears, ask yourself, 'What's the worst that could happen if I don't take this risk? What's the worst that could happen if I do?' Stratospheric leaders show that taking a chance on yourself can pay off.

As Rick shared, 'Sometimes, you just get a break along the way that allows you to find a new path and make something very powerful out of a business that could equally have failed.'

Failure or learning

Failure will happen. Maybe you are creating a service you want, but nobody else does. Maybe the market timing isn't right or you have invented the right product, but not calibrated it correctly. As a leader, you will sometimes find yourself on top of the world. Sometimes, you find yourself at the bottom.

As Rick candidly points out, 'We had three or four near-death experiences as a company.' Learning from failure is all about what you do in those moments. Do you allow those times to break you or define you?

The ability to absorb and manage failure is a necessary part of innovation. There will always be the seeds of success and learning to take away from every perceived failure. Lee speaks of 'the harder the day, the bigger the lesson', and often the failures are more important than the successes.

What I found interesting is the CEOs profiled in this book don't remember every success, but they do recall every one of their failures. For many people, it is too painful to go back and analyse failure, so they bury the event or outcome and don't learn from the experience. For stratospheric CEOs, it is the opposite. They confront the failures, they analyse them and sometimes, they can turn them upside down. Even if they can't, they take away an enormous number of lessons.

As Henry says, 'One failure is worth 1,000 lessons. You ask yourself, "What did we miss?", to ensure that failure never happens again. Most lessons from failures are common sense that isn't that common.'

Intuition versus analysis

How do you keep on risk taking, even the calculated risks, if there are going to be times when the bets go against you? As every good scientist knows, you need to create a hypothesis, and then test it, which is easier to do in a Petri dish than out in the real world.

Luckily, we do not exist in a vacuum. All the leaders I have worked with have carefully built highly capable and experienced teams who help them to test their hypotheses. They don't immediately go full steam ahead; instead, they go to their trusted advisors to get their input and expertise.

Next, they take the time to reflect and to question the idea again; to weigh the risk. When Lance is embarking on something new, he will always be asking himself and his team, 'What's the worst outcome? What if we fail in one aspect? What might we lose? What might we gain?' He challenges and tests the edges.

Rick and Michael also democratise the process and collect high-quality input. The greater the risk, the more they will seek input and data. This is not intended to enable a perfect decision, but to get them closer to making a better one. They usually know instinctively when something feels right, but by taking a moment to reflect and ask questions, and by listening to their confidants, they reduce the risk of failure.

Building and creating extraordinary companies is often underpinned by gut feelings. Analytical skills are a foundation, but you need to overlay your instincts and gut feelings on top to make good decisions. This requires you to teach your brain to listen to your instincts.

Gut feelings seldom come from nowhere – they are a distillation of all your experiences to date. Stratospheric CEOs listen to their gut instincts. They know when to pause and think, but they also know when to harness their instincts.

Henry shared, 'At business school, you initially learn how to build your analytical skills. You are taught how to analyse, how to be rational, and then you need to learn to let your instincts go wild.' This means listening to what your feelings are telling you; it's about taking risks that you cannot necessarily quantify in a spreadsheet.

Contrary to popular opinion, intuition *can* be built, honed and nurtured, but it takes practice. Lance says he honed his appetite for risk on the trading floor. Out there, every risk has a potential cost. If you keep count of when you listen to your gut and get it right, over a period, you'll develop the ability – and the innate confidence – to sense the risks that are worth taking.

Henry says that, over the millennia, it is gut instinct that has kept humans safe and allowed us to become the apex predators we are. Unfortunately, traditional education systems often try to squash our instincts. They teach us to ignore our deepest knowledge and regurgitate facts we have been taught. There is, of course, merit in learning facts, but we must do justice to our primal knowledge. The best education is the one that develops the brain and refines the instinct.

Momentum is key

Once Alex Honnold started climbing, there was no going back, no looking down – only forward momentum. If he lost pace on the wall of El Capitan, he would have lost his grip as well. When you are dealing with risk in business, you need the same momentum.

Lance explains that he never loses sleep over a risky decision. He makes the calls, he maintains his momentum, he trusts his gut, he acts.

For Alex to keep moving throughout his climb, he needed a perfect confluence of factors: weather, mental strength, physical agility and knowledge of every detail of the wall. Stratospheric CEOs also need a perfect combination of decision-making ability, a tried-and-true analytical framework, a team of trusted confidants, a gut instinct that has served them well and as many data points as they can muster.

Henry speaks of momentum often. You have to take a risk, because life is about small decisions that will add up to something worthy of the gamble. Sometimes it may be the wrong decision, but that's OK because you will react and recalibrate. You will take the next set of data, the next analysis, the next information and calculate for the next risk.

Summary

Risk tolerance can be learned. In spending time with stratospheric CEOs, I have found it is a characteristic they have honed until it is an intrinsic part of who they are. It's pervasive in everything they do.

Reflecting on their careers, the CEOs featured in this book recognise they are always seeking out the opportunities to use new technologies to gain a competitive advantage. They have risk-adjusted failure points that are higher than those of others because they're built on experience, and they have developed this trait.

As Lance shares, 'Over time, you get a track record of being more right than wrong, and, therefore, you gain confidence.'

Stratospheric leaders are the ones who don't lose sleep over the risky decisions. Their decision-making ability and their stomach for risk set them apart, allowing them to operate beyond the tolerance of most others.

As Lee says, 'You can't really be an entrepreneur unless you have a willingness to take risks.' Once you have tasted the emerging worlds, it's hard to go back, hence stratospheric leaders become serial entrepreneurs. Entrepreneurship transcends a career; it is a way of living and being.

As an entrepreneur, you want to move fast. You've got to make decisions and allow things to keep moving.

THREE

Execution

'Many people have ideas but spend all their time on their strategy. Execution is everything.'

Lance Uggla

Sitting at home, you may think it would be nice to have a new shelf. That's the easy bit. Sourcing, measuring, painting and fitting it is more challenging, and many shelves never make it all the way to the wall. Business is no different. Generating new ideas is simple; taking them on the long journey from conception to implementation is hard.

A vision without relentless execution is just a dream and attempting to execute without a vision is a mindless waste of time. Execution is the most important thing in any vision strategy. As Lance shares, 'You have to be willing to act.'

There are many entrepreneurs out there with transformative ideas and a great strategic vision, but who are unable to execute either.

They spend all their time on the strategy or fail to act. Combining strategic long-term thinking with rigorous execution year in and year out is a rare skill.

An idea only creates value when it becomes reality. As Henry Fernandez puts it, 'Get things done, get them done well, get them done on time, on budget while course correcting. That is the lifeblood of business.'

Rick McVey agrees that execution always wins the day. The idea must be appealing to your target market, but clients and investors don't reward people for talking about strategy. They want to see that you can demonstrate delivery, ie what have you done versus what you plan to get done. Saying what you are going to do and then doing what you say ultimately instils confidence and builds trust. Thoughts can only be great if you do something with them.

What, then, are the key things you need to be thinking about when it comes to execution?

Be an execution jockey and hire execution jockeys

The CEOs profiled in this book and their teams are what I call execution jockeys. It is one of their biggest strengths.

When you show you can execute your vision, it gives your collective stakeholders (especially your investors and potential customers) confidence. It also serves to attract more A players – people who want to be part of a winning team – which enables even stronger execution.

To identify those who can successfully execute your vision, looking for certain traits in the interview phase and drilling down through the curriculum vitae (CV) is critical. Does the candidate show excellent project-management skills? Can they develop and communicate a comprehensive plan? Can they pay attention to granular details? Do they have the flexibility to refine, modify or adapt to changing conditions as project implementation proceeds? Do they have the desire to collaborate and recognise the importance of doing do because execution is rarely an individual activity? This means assessing both what they have done physically *and* the methods they used.

Definable examples of these competencies will provide you with critical information on candidates' capabilities, their communication skills, their ability to manage connected parts, their proactive problem solving and leadership style. This enhances your probability of recruiting candidates with a track record of effective execution.

As you start thinking about execution, you need to bring other people in to problem solve and develop the ideation. As a leader, you don't have a monopoly on all the best ideas, which means being humble enough to know you don't have all the answers and curious enough to ask. It also requires you to be intentional about creating a diverse team that includes the constructive contrarians who will challenge your thinking and offer alternative views.

Clearly define and communicate your execution objectives

Execution of a successful vision requires something akin to tunnel vision or putting the horse blinkers on. It requires clearly defined objectives and a structured series of steps and pathways. Clarity will minimise any ambiguity.

Rick speaks of keeping it simple and narrowing the focus of what people need to do. 'If you give people a dozen things to do, the odds of them getting them all right go down. It's hard for them to know what to focus on.' Consequently, he concentrates his efforts on the most impactful actions in the execution of the strategy.

Lance speaks of the importance of focusing on one or two ideas, with quality winning over quantity: 'Don't focus on five to ten [ideas] because inevitably, you don't have the capability to execute at that level.' This can be a challenge for some leaders for whom the flow of great ideas is a superpower and a core strength. Relentless discipline and focus are the foundations of successful execution, which starts with the leader to ensure that the executive team concentrates on the critical few things rather than the trivial many.

Successful entrepreneurs are looking for the high watermark versus the average. The top investment/opportunity can be worth more than the total of all the others, and investment isn't just capital. Perhaps more importantly, it's teams investing their time, energy, effort and focus.

As you embark on your execution plan, there will be unknown unknowns. You can't possibly see the entire pathway at the start and things change over time with new information becoming available. Bringing new knowledge and insights into your decisions to enable iteration is a critical component to successful execution.

Constant, continual communication with your key internal and external stakeholders is important throughout execution of a vision. This ensures that all parties are updated, informed and engaged in the inevitable adjustments required. It also provides clarity on the success measures and mitigates the potential of mismatched expectations.

This essential feedback loop can be formal through meetings and periodic team reviews, or more informal through opportunities for general conversations. It gives you the ability to ensure that market sentiment, opinion and needs are continually assessed and marked against the decisions you are making.

The key questions to ask are, 'What is/isn't working? Are we on track? Where do we need to course correct?' Shane Akeroyd, former IHS Markit executive vice president, tells me that from an ongoing benchmarking perspective, the best leaders, such as Lance Uggla, will always be asking, 'What are we not doing?'

Rick meets with each of his senior executives a couple of times a week to understand how the teams' decisions are working out. Most leaders will tell you execution is hard as it requires multiple components across a product and market to be synthesised. Ongoing feedback where you actively engage and listen (with ears that hear) and you make, and empower others to make, the appropriate mid-course adjustments will ultimately give you better execution. The key is not to pontificate or be too slow to course correct if a change of direction is needed.

Keep your execution strategy simple in the long term, have clarity on what you want people to do and get constant feedback. The aim is to ensure the greatest amount of data to optimise knowledge. This in turn informs the next step and where best to allocate resources (team, time, capital) to have the greatest impact.

Discern between could and should

There is an opportunity cost to every minute of your time. Getting distracted by shiny objects will ultimately dilute your attention, and the attention of your management team and employees. Be discerning and differentiate between what *could* be done and what *should* be done.

Ruthlessly and relentlessly prioritising while learning to say no or not now is a superpower. Decisions ultimately only need to service and prioritise the designated goal.

When you're being asked to participate in events or calls or meetings, a key question to ask yourself is, 'Is this an enabler to achieving the big vision?' Conscious choice making in terms of where and how you invest your time will pay dividends.

One critical enabler is constant learning. The best leaders never stop learning. Rick credits the way he gathers information as a key to his success throughout his career. Some information he gathers in unplanned exchanges; the rest of his information gathering is focused and intentional. In most meetings, he prioritises it. He recognises the value of perspective and will engage regularly with those who can advance the big ideas.

He says, 'Every meeting, you can learn something.' He is always open to new inputs, to leveraging the experience, knowledge and insight of those around him.

This means being open, actively locked in and listening. Asking incisive questions coupled with active listening is a skill demonstrated by all the stratospheric leaders. Listening is an active behaviour, not a passive response, yet too often managers listen to respond rather than listening to learn, with two very different outcomes.

Lance agrees regarding the importance of the quality of your listening. It was something he really transitioned into in his forties, perfecting the talent in his fifties.

He offers, 'Many underestimate how important listening is. A lot of high-performance leaders are so excited about getting the decision moving faster, they are finishing sentences, they are thinking ahead, and as a result, they miss a whole bunch of things.' Information is one of the most important assets in any business, so all leaders could *and should* be listening to their people.

Gathering insight and information is without doubt what you should be doing, which means investing time in networking with the people who will be impacted by the decisions you make. Actively engage with clients and listen to what they want your business to be, and then build the tools to enable that. When businesses fail, it is often because the leaders have not understood their market (both how it operates today and, critically, how it can be innovated). They've not heard the market participants and have made product development an unconnected island. Meaningful disruption and innovation require multiple data threads continually adding, refining and modifying the framework of execution.

Be agile

Taking an idea and turning it into something tangible and profitable is not a linear path. No journey can begin with all the answers.

Success generally will be achieved not by doggedly following your first set of goals, but by your agility. Every project has dips or downturns; there will be corners to turn, hurdles to leap and obstacles to avoid. A stratospheric leader's job is to manage the team through these unknowns – to have the constant vision but regroup and re-strategise as needed. That is a differentiator.

Lance explains, 'It's a real leadership skill to stay positive. That needs to be practised.' It's the officer in the trenches motivating the troops; the cyclist who drags the peloton along in their draught.

According to his direct reports, Rick rallies the troops with, 'It might take a lot of work and it's going to take time, but we are going to take the hill.' When things don't go according to the plan, the leader is the one who communicates confidence and the ability to convert the hurdle or challenge into the execution pathway of the vision. Michael Spencer sees strategic objectives (which are laid out in the execution planning) as the key to accessing goals.

When Lance talks about the early days of Markit, he describes a process of micro-adjustment and iteration. He knew his original idea was sound. It had a purpose and a market. It had good customers: banks and asset managers who needed the product. Like software, though, a business needs resilient and sustainable flexibility.

He shares, 'You have a good idea, but as you start to develop more knowledge, don't be afraid to pivot.' This is increasingly pertinent given the rate of change led by tech-driven velocity. With Markit, Lance's vision was set, but the goals along the way remained malleable.

An open-minded leader continues to ask questions. They know what they want, but they are open to hearing opinions and advice, so they can learn and adjust. Sometimes, that means changing an approach or – less talked about – halting an idea or strategy while being able to reinvigorate it as needed.

Stephen Casper, lead director of MarketAxess, says:

> 'The first job of a leader is to make decisions with imperfect information. That's what ambiguity really is. Then being flexible enough to make tactical mid-course execution changes along the way without the long-term vision changing, which is a rare skill.'

Being open minded and allowing yourself to operate with imperfect information creates an attitude of agility, which is a key skill of stratospheric leaders and one they have consciously developed and harnessed. As one of Lance's peers shares, 'Lance is a person who's redefined himself and taught himself on the job. He's not afraid of digging in and figuring out, "What's right for now?" What was right for a start-up isn't necessarily right for the next phase.' These insights into agility enable you to continuously grow and evolve in how you're shaping your organisation.

Running a business of any size means juggling many moving parts. Talent will leave, market conditions will change, increased expectations will be placed on your shoulders, and you will invariably find yourself firefighting unforeseen events, often on a daily basis. If you lead and trailblaze, you *will* fail multiple times. There will be times when you feel that a day has simply involved treading water or even falling behind.

In moments like these, keep an eye on the end goal and your why (Sinek, 2011). Don't get discouraged and remind yourself that when you're innovating and pushing boundaries, failing is a feature. Aside from its huge potential for learning, failure is another opportunity to hone your agility.

The straight path to success is a myth, yet to the outside world, the success stratospheric leaders have achieved seems straightforward. Most people see the visible: the accolades, the market share, the industry rankings, the polls. Others are not usually invited to see the multiple personal sacrifices and the minefields they've successfully navigated. Leadership takes mental and physical strength to keep moving forward; to get back up and keep going.

Challenges, setbacks, detours, speedbumps, curveballs, distractions and irritations should be expected. Setbacks are in fact a feature of execution, not a bug. Seeing them as components in the execution roadmap, learning and adapting to them, rather than seeing them as failure or incapability is the key to stratospheric leadership.

Surf often, snorkel sometimes, scuba by appointment

If you have been intentional about hiring people who, as Henry says, 'can get things done', as a leader, you should have the confidence to step away from the day-to-day execution to focus on the strategy. This requires trust in the talent around you, zooming in only when required.

Brad Levy, CEO of Symphony (a network and communication platform aimed at the financial markets) and an expert sounding board for me throughout the writing of this book, refers to this process as the three S's: surf, snorkel and scuba. As a leader, you should surf by nature, snorkel regularly to look below the surface while recognising when to scuba for the deeper dive. Operating at a high level (surfing) will require you to build processes to enable this, from meeting structures to how information flows more generally.

One of the attributes that make stratospheric CEOs unique is their ability to operate on multiple levels. They are involved in the deep dives when necessary, but they don't get lost there. If you are scuba diving for too long, you might miss the world changing above you or storms on the horizon. As a leader, you never want to be blindsided while underwater.

Be deliberate in measuring progress

It was well-known management consultant Peter F Drucker who said, 'What is measured improves' (Drucker, 2006). Stratospheric leaders have a clear execution plan and are deliberate about measuring progress regularly against their goals and budget to see it visually, graphically, in a spreadsheet or through numbers. As the unknowns become known, they then make the necessary changes as they go.

This means measuring the right things and not vanity metrics, which don't give a true reflection and so will be providing a false narrative. For Lance, execution is all about the things that lead to your desired outcome. Getting those right is so important. If you want sales revenue to go up 10%, measuring sales revenue every day is measuring the outcome, but what are the inputs to achieve it? How many calls is each salesperson making? How many customer proposals are being sent out? What are the results in your customer satisfaction surveys? All are indicators of how customer orientated your team is.

Deliberate intention in measuring leading indicators of the team's control and ability to influence will increase the probability of success. Don't be blinkered. Going through easy macro cycles gives many leaders a false sense of achievement. It can create confidence based on helium and safety nets. Asset bubbles come and go and people themselves can inflate and ex/implode.

How willing are you to measure yourself against the execution?

Exercise patient urgency

Keep the long-term goal in mind. This is what Rick McVey shares about his company's long-term goal:

> 'The things we were saying about why we started
> MarketAxess in 2002, we are still saying today. We're
> here to build great technology to help our fixed-income
> clients trade in a radically more efficient way, lowering
> transaction costs and creating new liquidity.'

There are generally few executives who take the long-term view of the world, particularly in financial services – an industry that tends to have such a debilitating short-term focus. The one-year budget or plan is often the problem. It's about the next bonus, the next quarter, the next meeting with an investor.

For some people, planning towards a goal that could be decades away seems ridiculous, but as Brad Levy says:

> 'Life without the long view can look pretty short. You
> have to have the three-year vision, the one-year plan, and

measure hard every ninety days. The attention to three years and ninety days simultaneously is key – long-term vision broken down into shorter-term execution cycles. This will allow you to listen to where you are going wrong or may be too early.'

Any shorter than ninety days and you don't build in enough time to win. You have to have the long three-year vision as your compass and the short ninety-day execution.

Stratospheric leaders want to achieve their goal. They want it tomorrow, but they recognise that the big things take time and it's the many small things that add up.

As Michael shares, 'In the heat of battle, when everyone around is driving forward, there are times when a leader's greatest power is often the pause.' Without reflection, knee-jerk reactions can drive you off course. Is a blip a one-off? Is it exceptional? How representative is it? Are patterns and themes emerging? Are there wider issues or challenges in the execution strategy? These are a few examples of the questions you could pause to ask. It's what you do with this information and fresh insight that matters. Moving forwards requires you to turn your knowledge into action.

The US Navy SEALs have a maxim: 'Slow is smooth and smooth is fast' (Brinkman, 2019). To execute a plan with the precision of the elite military, you will succeed quickly if you do so in a way that is conscious, deliberate and focused. Going slow is about deliberate focus and conscious movement. There are times when slowing down with intention and purpose will help you make sound, high-impact decisions and maintain emotional balance. Crucially, it will also reduce your and your team's chances of burning out.

Remember Isaac Newton's third law of motion (Newton, 1687): 'To every action there is an equal and opposite reaction'. Acting too fast can create greater resistance. An M&A is a case in point. Buying a company is one thing; executing a smooth and successful integration is another.

According to Lance, an M&A transaction is exactly when adopting a slower or more moderate pace based on empathy for those affected can yield dividends. It may seem counterintuitive to slow down, but that may be the right way to accelerate towards completion. The personal touch means a sympathetic onboarding, which supports a successful execution.

'Lucky' execution

All the leaders profiled in this book attribute a portion of their success to luck – the families they were born into, their upbringing and the opportunities that set the trajectory of their lives. Although he, like all the stratospheric CEOs, has immense gratitude for his position, Lance shares that it's good to allow yourself to pause every once in a while, to pinch yourself and go, 'Geez, I'm really lucky to be here.'

Although there are occasional bolts from the universe that enable magic to occur, serendipity is more often a culmination of multiple threads of execution – both the physical and the mental. The discipline, the hard work, the agility, the courage and the fortitude all add up to create what can be seen as luck.

Stratospheric leaders can take these components and enable them in others (or have the ability to convince others they have them). This is called emotional contagion. Examples of emotional contagion occur daily – like when you see somebody smile, that usually invokes a smile in response and causes, even fleetingly, something positive to occur within you. The same is true of qualities such as discipline and courage and fortitude. These can also be contagious.

Influencing teams, clients, stakeholders is a critical component of execution – the ability to communicate and convince a market of the possibility of the impossible is contagious. This skill, which is based on a set of attitudes, can be learned and is available to all of us, but it's not always exercised. Thinking we're lucky rarely converts to us being lucky, but the required mental skills of execution give us more power than we may think we have to create an environment of serendipity.

The expansive outlook of stratospheric leaders, their ability to spot and seize opportunities and the way they build relationships add up to a superpower. Many people who have had an equally good start in life desire success. Few are in for the long haul and even fewer are prepared to do what it takes to get there.

Celebrate the wins

If you execute successfully on your vision, the benefits multiply – you win, your team wins, your investors win. You create a track record that brings with it confidence and belief.

It's important to acknowledge and celebrate the mini wins and the significant moments along the execution journey. It is easy to be looking forward all the time and to live in a world of next-ing, immediately moving on to the next audacious goal. Lance is always asking, 'What's the next thing?' This is the zone stratospheric leaders inhabit, which I see as a double-edged sword.

The positive side is, it has driven them to realise their stratospheric goals and never miss the next big thing coming. You don't want the wins today to trap you tomorrow, but you should be taking time every now and then to step back and reflect on your achievements. This doesn't mean driving the car while looking in the rear-view mirror. It does mean taking a moment to enjoy the journey.

The celebration of your achievements need not be a big direct debit of time, braggadocio, overt or 'look at me'. It could be a personal reflection to harvest the success. Ask yourself, 'What do I want to celebrate about myself in having achieved this goal?' After all, there will have been many inputs to get to the outcome. Another question may be, 'If I was to do it all again, how would I improve on the execution next time?' Celebrate where you've got to while adopting a growth mindset and applying the learnings to future endeavours.

Rick and his team are intentional about acknowledging how important clients have been to supporting their vision. One of the MarketAxess tag lines is 'We created open trading, but our clients created the marketplace'. They celebrate the client backing and those who have shown great confidence and really believed in them, which is what has got them to where they are.

Acknowledging your teams' and clients' contributions in executing the strategy to achieve the goal is a valuable motivational opportunity. Don't underestimate the power of a few words of heartfelt recognition.

Customer-centric focus

Unquestionably one of the most important sections in this chapter is this one. If you are customer centric, this means constantly engaging your customers in your product development. It means seeing them as partners and actively investing in and valuing your relationships with them. As I reflect on my conversations with the CEOs and how they speak about their customers, I see a common thread: they aren't seeking to answer the question, 'What is good for me?' Instead, they ask, 'What is good for us?'

A customer's experience of you and your business is key. Lance shares, 'If you want to be successful, focus on customer satisfaction and engagement. It won't happen all by itself.' For Lance, it's about motivating the team to be customer orientated and being deliberate about measuring this. Rick's approach is to 'build distinctive technology that will matter to clients and provide world-class client service'.

Regular interaction with clients keeps stratospheric leaders tapped into the market. It keeps their businesses relevant, and it offers valuable and different perspectives. Ongoing feedback feeds into stratospheric leaders' love of learning and continuous improvement. It also helps them validate their ideas.

Stratospheric leaders' teams speak of them being the first to pick up the phone to an important client when there is an issue. When you face problems head on rather than trying to hide from them, it demonstrates you value the client and care about the relationship. This subsequently offers you latitude and grace when dealing with tension or challenges.

Networks and relationships are not about who you know, but about who knows you. Developing a meaningful client network takes time because underpinning all successful relationships is trust. This means doing what you say, delivering on promises, operating with integrity, being transparent and making people feel valued and appreciated. Simple to do, yet rarely executed well.

Summary

New ideas are the beating heart of entrepreneurialism; hence many stratospheric leaders are obsessed with the question, 'What's next?' You must be able to recognise the good ideas, though, as not every idea can go the whole way.

Innovation drives the energy of the company, but to be successful, leaders and their teams must have discipline around execution. A well laid-out execution plan within the strategy and a willingness to measure yourself and your teams against it, plus the agility to pivot where necessary, plus a relentless focus brings your vision into reality.

Constantly looking for the next audacious goal is great, but be sure to make time to celebrate the little wins as well as the big ones. Remember to acknowledge everyone who has contributed to the successful execution of the vision – the teams and the customers. The business leader who shows they respect and value their customers is the one who is already on a journey into the stratosphere.

Global Crisis Management

'The secret of managing a crisis is halting the downward spiral before it gains momentum.'

Lee Olesky

In 1606, an outbreak of plague reached Shakespeare's hometown. He decided to self-isolate and, home alone, he wrote *King Lear* and *Macbeth* (Shapiro, 2015).

We can't always predict and plan for external events ahead. It's what we choose to do in moments of crisis that matters. What is the attitude, mindset, leadership of self and others we choose to bring? How can we in fact leverage the crisis and, like Shakespeare, turn it into an opportunity?

What is a crisis? Our modern interpretation of the word is akin to 'catastrophe' or 'emergency'. The word 'crisis', however, comes from the ancient Greek *krisis*, meaning 'decision'. In other words, it's a moment where an opportunity can be grasped or lost.

Every one of our stratospheric leaders has experienced decisive and defining moments: the rise of the internet; the dotcom bubble bursting; the advent of the euro; 9/11; the banking collapses of 2008; the Covid pandemic. Today's world is stressful. For years we have been dealing with existential threats to our businesses and our lives. From pandemics to international relations to climate change, we live in fear at least some of the time. Heightened disruption is the new normal. Change is acute, pervasive and exponential.

Today's dynamic, complex global landscape can leave us firefighting unforeseen events. It requires a different level of resilience to be able to bounce back. In times of global crisis, the stratospheric leader shows courage and foresight.

Leading through heightened disruption and exponential change is now an inevitable part of modern-day leadership as our environments face multiple buffeting winds. This at times requires highly situational and adaptive approaches. Your resources will be tested. It is more likely than not that yesterday's playbook won't navigate tomorrow's challenges.

It's a certain type of leader and human being who can successfully navigate through uncharted territory and thrive in times of crisis. Bringing direction and instilling calm amid chronic chaos is a superpower, so what are the golden rules I have learned from the stratospheric leaders in terms of the *what* and the *how* of leadership when you're faced with crisis events?

Don't panic

There will always be global market-moving events – wars, pandemics, financial crises are scattered throughout history. Henry

Fernandez shares, 'As a leader, you know the difficult times will come. It's just a question of when.'

In crisis events, stratospheric leaders are not looking around to see what everyone else is doing. Instead, they are making quick decisions that are focused on their market, their business and their people. They are then taking the immediate learnings, the new data points, and adapting. Their nimbleness and learning in real time is key.

As a leader, you are required to make crisis decisions and operate with imperfect and incomplete information. Yet leaders are often unfairly judged through the lens of hindsight when more becomes known. Making the right decisions in the moment requires internal checks and balances to determine whether they are considered responses or knee-jerk reactions.

Some good questions to ask yourself are:

- What is my decision-making state at this moment relative to the challenge?

- What am I noticing?

- How am I reacting?

- What are the facts?

- What information is available to me? What might I be missing?

- Have I dealt with something similar before? What did I do? What was the result?

- How do I need to be in this moment to get to the best outcome?

- Whose voice(s) would I benefit from listening to?

It can be hard making critical decisions under duress and pressure. The ability to manage impulse and filter out unnecessary distractions is key. If you find yourself in a reactive state, you are unlikely to be in the strongest position to make effective decisions, which is where enlisting the help of others is advised. It will enable you to separate yourself from the immediate problems. Leadership is about mastery of the mind and not just technical prowess.

Michael Spencer had to employ his own golden 'don't panic' rule during 9/11. ICAP had people in both the Twin Towers. Luckily, they all got out safely, but ICAP lost its entire US operations and back-up systems.

When the markets reopened a week later, ICAP's share price had halved. Michael felt the existential risk to the firm, asking himself, 'Are we going to be able to survive this?'

Rather than panic, he took action, flying to New York, borrowing facilities from Bloomberg and assembling a small crisis-management team around him. He took responsibility for North America and for the recovery of the business, and told everyone else to roll up their sleeves and focus on their respective regions. Within a couple of months, ICAP had a skeletal operational state in the US. A year later, you would never have known the real jeopardy that faced the organisation. ICAP had more than recovered.

In hindsight, Michael learned that a business can face enormous threats, world-changing events, and still survive. It's all about what you do in those moments. His approach: 'Do the right thing; don't prevaricate; make the right decisions calmly and thoughtfully and don't delay.'

Chris Willcox agrees. 'In these moments, follow the basics. Be calm. Be rational and don't get panic struck.'

Lance Uggla understands the importance of stepping back to formulate a sensible response. As he shared with his team at the start of the Covid pandemic and the subsequent global lockdowns, 'We can't change what has just happened. We will be measured on how we respond.'

Staying calm, focused and level-headed is part of a stratospheric leader's unique formula. You don't want to exacerbate the emotional contagion. Lee Olesky says:

> 'As a leader, you have responsibility to take action and people need direction. This means blocking other things out, so you can focus on asking, "What are we going to do?", and then you need to prioritise and delegate, so people know who is responsible for what and they have clarity of their role.'

The biggest crisis event of the twenty-first century so far has been Covid-19. Many regarded it as an unprecedented moment in world history, but if history teaches us anything, it's that nothing is new and no challenge is unique. This is why stratospheric leaders are all voracious learners, especially from those that have gone before them. What did former leaders do when confronted with a crisis? How did they react? What was their philosophy? How did they manage the process? Stratospheric CEOs then use the knowledge gleaned from these questions to inform their own decision making.

Control what you can control

Life will always throw challenging events our way. We are defined by the way we respond. Do we withdraw and become resigned, or do we draw a line between the factors we can and can't control and get resourceful?

Being a modern leader means that we sacrifice a degree of control. The aircraft pilot can't influence the weather or the density of air traffic, but they can adapt to them. They can ensure that the mood on board the plane is positive and calm. They can listen to the co-pilot and ground control to make the right decisions.

Like the pilot during a flight, stratospheric business leaders need to calibrate. What do you need to remain in control of? What can you let go?

As highlighted by clergyman and author Charles Swindoll through the title of his book, *Life Is 10% What Happens to You and 90% How You React* (Swindoll, 2023), there are many things outside of your control, given the unpredictable nature of events. You can, however, control your response, attitude and mindset. That is within your capabilities and something you can be responsible for. This means giving thought to the energy you are radiating out. Pausing and taking a breath will help you deal with all those stress-invoking situations.

Perhaps the biggest danger facing leaders is the few moments of calm. How does the pilot react when the flight is smooth with no evidence of turbulence ahead? As Michael Spencer warns, no matter how good things are, 'Never get complacent. Never take anything for granted.'

Assemble a small crisis-management team

We will speak about the importance of the team in Chapter Five, but it is worthy of a mention here. The people around you in times of crisis will strongly influence how you come through them. At those times, stratospheric leaders bring together a small, select group with different vantage points and perspectives to help determine the best approach, strategy and response, given the information available.

Rick McVey made the decision early on to expand his management team in line with the expansion of the business, because 'the more great heads you have when there's a crisis, the better off the organisation will be'. This foresight isn't just about crisis readiness; it's about leadership and board proactivity in the face of potential threats like artificial intelligence, climate change or cyberattacks, and having a group of experts you can engage with, ensuring swift and effective responses.

This means as a leader recognising that your previous knowledge and experience may carry less weight in certain events. It requires you to acknowledge what you don't know and be comfortable asking for input where needed. Diverse skillsets and experiences within the crisis-management team serve as a powerful reservoir of potential solutions.

Chris says that in crisis moments, you may be asking people to take on tasks outside their normal realm of responsibility, so as a leader, you must accept that people will make mistakes. Your teams need to know that you are providing the air cover and will take responsibility for the decisions they're making, especially if they are later challenged or seen to be misaligned. Show that if people do what you need them to do, you will support them through any potential negative consequences. This is critical to further empower the team around you and mitigate the hesitation that can arise in moments that require a decision.

Decision making in the grey zone

As the leader, you will be required to make decisions, often with tight timescales, under pressure and in the spotlight. Chris says it's here that you have to make a judgement call as to how damaging making a wrong decision would be. There are some decisions that have irreversible consequences, so must be taken with incredible due diligence – these are known as one-way door decisions, since they can't be easily reversed. Then there are two-way door decisions, where the door opens both ways and, if they don't work out, you can undo them without much damage being done.

The first thing that you need to figure out is which decisions are irreversible and which decisions can be quickly changed if they turn out to be wrong. The reality is in a crisis, while it's your responsibility to communicate your decisions, there can be room for forgiveness and flexibility granted to you around the decision itself. Reasonable stakeholders understand that the due diligence that goes into decision making can't take as long or be as deep in times of a crisis.

Everybody has their principles for decision making, but it's challenging to execute under pressure. Things are generally much harder to get right than people think. Lance is always looking at the long-term impact of decisions on the business, thinking about customers, employees and shareholders. He is not making decisions for just one of those groups, but for the company so that they will best support all three.

Successful leaders possess or have cultivated a capacity and understand the need for making tough choices (often unpopular ones) in stressful moments – staying composed, focused and deliberate. They have learned to show courage and act with conviction. Not always easy, but a necessary part of leadership.

Be visible

In times of crisis, leaders are required to acknowledge the situation while walking a tightrope. They can say too much, use language which easily offends, or alternatively say too little, which is taken as them not caring. The key thing is to be neither too loud nor too quiet as a leader, but you do need to say something.

Here's a list of tips from the stratospheric CEOs:

- Acknowledge the situation.

- Recognise and connect with those impacted.

- Anticipate a potential backlash if you leave it too long before you communicate.

- Show empathy. Don't underestimate the impact to those affected by a situation or decision. When you speak from the heart, you will connect with the heart.

- Go human and lead from the caring gene. When the corporate voice kicks in too much, the message gets diluted and sounds inauthentic.

- Create multiple forums and keep communication constant.

- Keep written communication short and succinct to mitigate risk of misunderstanding.

- Understand that getting your communication perfectly right isn't a realistic benchmark. Just aim not to get it terribly wrong.

- It's OK to admit to the limitations of your knowledge. Invite those impacted by the crisis to educate you.

Chris shares that your people will value honesty and thoughtfulness. During Covid, there were many examples of executives with their beach house in the background on video calls, which ultimately didn't project the message 'we are all in this together'. It leads to an incongruence of words versus behaviours.

Chris believes the more uncertainty your teams are presented with, the more they will value being informed, advising, 'Tell them the truth even if it is uncomfortable.' Unequivocal positivity isn't authentic or real, but in times of distress, providing a balance to the intensity of the reality and shifting the conversation to the future, including the immediate future (ie tomorrow), will allow for perspectives to adjust. Even a minor shift to an alternative future-looking reality has value as it will, in that moment, allow for a reprieve from the immediate crisis.

Where appropriate, keep your stakeholders informed about how decisions are made. Be OK with communicating uncomfortable truths and prepared to sacrifice short-term morale by telling the truth versus communicating unrealistic perceptions.

Perception can become reality, so intentionality around people's experience of you is critical. Put yourself in their shoes to understand the key components of the message and how others will feel about it. If you are able to direct people and assuage their uncertainty, you enable morale to rapidly regenerate and new realities to become the status quo.

Exercise behavioural range

People are always looking at you as a leader and this amplifies in times of crisis, when your words, actions and behaviours are all exposed and analysed. Those around you want to understand how you *really* feel about the situation.

Most people prefer certainty over chaos. The unexpected can drive anxiety and fear. At that time, people in organisations look to leaders for confidence, calmness, control and a sense of 'we've got this'.

As Lee shares, 'Even though you could be going through a stressful time yourself, people are counting on you.'

Chris agrees. 'Your people want to know the person steering the ship is competent.'

There is the what and the how of leadership – what you do in moments of crisis and how you do it. What is the energy you are using to convey your message? How do people experience you when you walk into the room? The first thirty words and the first thirty seconds of your message will strongly influence the feeling of those you are speaking to. This means giving thought to your desired outcome. What information do you want them to leave with? How do you want them to feel? Knowing that, how do you need to be?

I call this behavioural range.

We have many levers available to us as leaders, including the tone of our voice, active listening, eye contact, our calmness of presence, our desire to understand somebody else's experience, openness and honesty in our communication. Behavioural range is knowing which ones to dial up or down in a given situation to have the impact we want to create.

Tough times can be the differentiators

Not every black swan event is a disaster. Henry shares:

'It's in tough times when we have added the most value to our company, when we have done our biggest acquisitions. It is in the tough times when we have picked up the best talent, hired the best people. It is in the tough times when we have come up with more innovation.

When you aggregate it, it's where you can make the quantum leaps ahead of the competition, because they don't want to take risks.'

Rick speaks of the regulatory reform in response to the financial crisis. He recognised with this permanent change in regulation, the financial world was going to need a new business model for credit trading, which is when MarketAxess promoted all-to-all trading (dealers plus investors) way ahead of anybody else as part of the solution.

The introduction of all-to-all trading was initially met with opposition from dealers because it disintermediated them – traders did not have to use them to find the other side of a trade. Before, dealers would take a relatively large markup to provide this service, but all-to-all trading allows two counterparties to trade with each other electronically.

Over time, though, the dealers used the MarketAxess system for small, low-touch trading while reserving their high-touch service for their larger clients, becoming more profitable than they were before. That was validation for Rick and his team of trusting in your response and pre-empting the solutions your clients need.

A decade or so earlier, Michael saw the rise of the euro as a pivotal moment in the way and scale that trading systems could work, and he exploited that moment. For Henry, Covid was a time to connect with his clients, his team and his investors. None of this was new – Henry has always been the kind of man who values the importance of face time, but moving to virtual meetings allowed him to do this more frequently, breaking tradition and remaking it for the new landscape in the post-pandemic world.

Lance too used the Covid period to pivot and evolve. He looked at what his business could deliver digitally and online, seeking out new ways to connect with his clients. In four weeks, he and his team built a content platform to share research. The goal wasn't to sell more, it was to get as many clients using and consuming the company's research and analytics as possible – absolutely free.

While salespeople might not like the free-of-charge model, helping your customers out at a time of crisis – providing them with solutions without profiting yourself – is how you build loyalty for the long term. Clients will remember who stood by them, and this in turn engenders trust and strengthens relationships. Stratospheric CEOs are seasoned businesspeople, so even the perception of doing right is what is right for the business.

As Henry says, 'You have a responsibility to the opportunity.' For Lee, this means regenerating your company every year into one that is better. It can't just do what it used to do. It's your ability to course correct and adjust and leverage the opportunity of tough times that will set you apart.

Rick says, 'You don't hide from the issue; you don't deny the issue is there. You face up to it and try as much as you can to play it to your advantage.'

Henry describes business as being a boat. If conditions are calm and the tide is rising, it's hard to differentiate. It's in the stormy seas where you can stand out.

Good business requires empathy

A generation ago, when people were asked about the qualities they look for in a leader, 'empathy' would rarely have been an attribute mentioned. However, modern-day leadership requires us to be more human, and empathy is not only a superpower, it's also a key requirement. It brings out the best in people, which ultimately is good for business.

Empathy means having the ability to understand the feelings of others, or at least communicating the perception of that understanding. When the pandemic locked us into our homes, leaders who had always been office based had to adapt. Lockdown was mandated and a no-choice situation. Embracing new ways of working was hard for everyone and foreign to their experience, but the strongest leaders were those who were quick to figure out the challenges their people were facing. Covid was an equalising event (even the richest were cleaning their own bathrooms), so the leader's ability to adapt to the realities of their teams was critical to keep the lights on.

In *To Kill a Mockingbird*, Harper Lee's Atticus Finch teaches us to walk a mile in someone else's shoes to really understand their perspective (Lee, 1960). Henry advocates something similar. He says that only through listening can we learn. This means being curious to understand what people are really thinking and feeling, getting insight into what they are worrying about. It's not just about what they say, but the messaging in their unsaid words too.

Empathy needs to be perceived to be real. There may be times as a leader where you don't have the reserves of energy to care deeply about everything. After all, you are not immune to the events impacting your people, but in these moments, you still have to act as if you do care. If your people merely get a sense of platitudes, it will work against you.

As the title of leadership coach Marshall Goldsmith's excellent book tells us, *What Got You Here Won't Get You There* (Goldsmith, 2008). A human-centric approach is critical for the effective modern-day leader. It will drive the reality and perceptions of your leadership. You have to care or at least be seen to care.

Although our leaders recognise the importance and impact of empathy and care (which were both prevalent in their upbringings), they are also tough and demanding, have strong opinions and will push people hard. These qualities can co-exist and the combination, dealt out in appropriate doses to align with the moment, is what will have the most significant impact and consequence.

Chris shares:

> 'If you are a good leader, you will have a store of goodwill you can draw upon in times of crisis. In these moments, you may not have a formula to follow, but your behaviours and actions pre-crisis will determine how your team responds to the demands you put upon them.'

Summary

Stratospheric leaders develop the capacity to face what seem to be insurmountable crises and convert them into opportunities to create value, driving loyalty and new directions. Effectively, they leverage the challenge.

The ability to navigate often global events requires emotional strength and resilience and the capacity to think clearly, above the actual immediacy of the situation, about the business – its people, its customers and its product. Knowledge of each of those and leadership around them ultimately enables the stratospheric leader to get through the changes and challenges and thrive.

FIVE

Leading Others

'Leadership is a fortunate position to be in,
and therefore you need to find ways to keep
lifting people up, not pushing them back.'

Lance Uggla

As children, we are repeatedly told about the importance of learning and scholarly achievement, of gaining skills and qualifications. This is all in the expectation that expertise and success will follow.

Many successful people spend up to a quarter of their lives within the education system, gathering more letters after their names and ever-lengthening CVs. Without question, there are critical thresholds and merits related to this, but leadership is generally not a skill taught across pre-tertiary education systems. Yet it is ultimately the most critical component in driving professional success.

Stratospheric leaders are intentional about building incredible teams to support the culture, innovation and ideals of their businesses.

People, their endeavours and their intellectual capability, curiosity and contributions are the most valuable assets in any organisation. Every product, decision, strategy needs a leader, a team and the value they create.

An African proverb states, 'It takes a village to raise a child', conveying the message it takes many people (the village) to provide a safe, healthy environment, where children are given the security they need to develop and flourish. This is not dissimilar to growing a business. Behind every great leader is a great team, and for you as a leader, this means bringing people with you.

Perhaps the most challenging action for you as a leader will be releasing the structural reins of direct control, so how do you build out the teams that you can trust to carry forward your message, product and strategy? In turn, how do they then elevate themselves to lead from a higher level with greater impact?

Assemble a world-class leadership team

In any level of business, scaling successfully is unlikely to be a result of providence, happenstance or accident. Instead, scale is achieved through careful cultivation. While there is always a risk of birds of a feather flocking together, the strongest of leaders usually have a level of awareness of their own limitations and blind spots (and in small, trusted groups, they admit to them).

Our stratospheric leaders generally surround themselves with individuals who have different skills, views, opinions, styles and backgrounds. This clearly enables broader perspectives and allows for more balanced decisions.

Rick McVey says, 'This diversity of opinion, thought, skills and experience brings power to decision making.' It is also a necessity for a reflective, self-aware leader looking to ensure that decisions are being based on a wide range of views and opinions. Anything less in today's world would, in Rick's opinion, be suboptimal.

MarketAxess is highly intentional in its hiring process. Rick and his team refer to it as 'Assembling the Avengers' – a metaphor that is critical in business as ultimately, teams need to be structured and optimised for the strengths and skills required in a particular organisation or for a particular product. Combining skills and expertise has the potential to create a unique chemistry, which if successfully implemented and directed raises the bar, elevates the energy in the room and enables a lighthouse effect out to the wider organisation.

I've used the word *intentionality* many times throughout the book, to emphasise that for our stratospheric CEOs, success is for the greater part by design. Intentionality also applies to how they hire. They actively seek out those people who have the skills, expertise and knowledge to be key players in scaling and building out the business, as well as being the required cultural fit.

It can be costly (in time and money) to make the wrong hiring decisions, yet it does happen. Lance takes a highly tactical approach to hiring. First, he looks for engagement, asking, 'Do I like the energy this person brings to the room?' For him, this is a key attribute as the capital markets ecosystem is an 'insider' market, so the ability to create and cultivate relationships is a fundamental requirement.

A close second is demonstration of ability, intellectual skills and attributes, which includes approaches to and actual hands-on problem solving. Third comes the all-important career arc question: 'Does this person see a forward trajectory with my team, or are they here to learn and leave? Ultimately, do they see a future path for themselves within my organisation?'

Often, leaders prioritise the second point – looking for the intellectual skills. Whether consciously or unconsciously, Lance focuses on what he has determined to be the overarching attribute (energy and engagement) and that is the foundational hurdle critical to a hire. Without that, the other components do not even rise to the level of consideration.

Of course, underpinning all of that is reflection – the ability to think about the person, the team and the business to ensure that the qualities and attributes that are being added will enable a broader perspective. Does this person bring a new context, experience and opinion? For Lance, a balanced firm is a better firm.

Henry Fernandez is a believer in balancing home-grown talent with acquired talent. If you only hire from outside, what is the message you are giving your team members about their skills and qualities? If you only hire from within, where is your diversity? Where do fresh ideas and concepts come from? As with Lance, intentionality underpins the shape and evolution of Henry's teams. This requires him to think about the bigger picture and not just the immediate requirements of the role.

Like many old adages, 'success begets success', while far too general, has its foundation rooted in truth. In the context of business, people like to win and want to be associated with other winners. Successful teams bring ambitious, driven, smart people together to create greater success. Add to that the elements of inspiration and innovation that come with working alongside other A players and together, they create an intoxicating formula for stratospheric success.

The more successful you become, the more successful people you attract. You need to be aiming to hire for where you want to be (ie more successful than today), to help further this flywheel.

Get to know your team

It was Aristotle who said, 'Knowing yourself is the beginning of all wisdom', and equally true is knowing the people you work alongside. The more you know about a person, the more you can trust them. By getting to know how people tick, you have their markers and can move them along or upward. Understanding their motivations and drivers allows you as the leader to connect to the part of yourself that is going to resonate best with that person.

Lance mentioned an exercise he uses to establish how invested managers are in getting to know their people. He asks them to write the names down of all their reports. Next to each name, he asks managers to note whether they are married or in a relationship and then, if relevant, asks for their partner's name. Do they have any children? How old are they? Finally, he asks managers to write down three interests their people have, such as sports, music, hobbies.

Ahead of doing the exercise, nearly everyone in a room would raise their hand to confirm they know their team members well, yet in his experience, nine out of ten have quite a few 'don't knows' on their sheet of paper by the end. They don't know their people's personal circumstances, even though they work with them every day. They have taken little interest in the person, and this is one of the biggest mistakes you can make as a leader. You can be the smartest person in the room, but if you can't take others on the journey with you, it will ultimately limit your level of success.

People will invest in you if they believe that you are invested in them, and you show that through truly getting to know them. If you are transactional in your approach to how you manage your people, that is how they will respond.

If you were to take a moment now, how well do you really know the people who work for you? Not at the surface level, but the real stuff.

Once you have gathered your Avengers and made the effort to get to know them, you then need to harness their strengths to help them thrive. Henry shared a story of spending the holiday period with his children, teaching them about human nature. He said that every human has strengths and weaknesses, and it is much more beneficial to focus on harnessing their strengths instead of fighting their weaknesses.

This is a critical point for Henry. Actually *seeing* the human inside the individual enables him to grow and nurture a team more effectively. By thoughtfully putting people into roles that will allow their strengths to shine, he ensures those individuals and the team are performing at more ambitious levels – which in turn feeds into the success of the company.

He demonstrates this mindset in performance reviews. Rather than focusing on the 10% of things the person doesn't do well, Henry instead invests 90% of the time on the things they excel at, the idea being that the person becomes so good at those things, whatever they don't do well doesn't matter.

'I spend a huge amount of time explicitly thinking about a person's attributes,' he says. 'About what they're good at, rather than what they're not good at.'

Harnessing people's strengths also means creating the right environment for them to thrive. Consider this analogy: when a plant fails to grow, do we find fault in the flower, or do we scrutinise the environment in which it is grown? Does it receive sufficient light, air and water? Are the surrounding weeds removed? Is there enough space for the roots to expand? Has there been sufficient pruning to stimulate growth? Individuals, like plants, require optimal conditions to thrive. As a leader, fostering this conducive environment is paramount.

Don't be afraid to make changes

Talent is the difference between taking a motorway versus taking the winding country roads to reach a destination. With a great team, you can make the road wider and smoother, reaching your destination faster with fewer obstacles along the way.

Having a great team means hiring the best people you can and pruning and cultivating the skills the business needs. As it grows, the business will need different skills in different seats at different stages, which may mean moving people around and letting others go.

As you evaluate the positions your business needs at a given time, there is an opportunity to look at the skills you have amassed across the broader group. It makes sense to move your most talented people into the highest-yielding opportunities, placing them where there is a skills match or where the individual has a high learning potential. If your people trust you, they will trust that you are making the right decisions for them.

Stratospheric leaders have figured out their business, their product and their market. The challenge then is to really understand the skills and capabilities of their teams and to have the confidence to move people around to unlock potential – a synonym for what is right for the business. This ultimately keeps people motivated and inspired.

Lee Olesky shares, 'Giving people an opportunity can be a serious motivator and will pay back in multiples in terms of commitment and drive.' Many of the leaders featured in this book estimate a minimum of 20% of their time is spent focused on people management.

Lance is considered by those around him to be excellent at measuring an individual's natural talents. He has learned this by observing behaviour, actions and expressions, listening to their questions, their language. He then seeks to build on what he's learned.

So often in leadership, people look at the responses of an individual as the arbiters of talent. Exceptional leaders are looking for more – the thought processes behind the words, the body language and, critically, what is unsaid and nuanced. They soon recognise the pretenders.

Lance is also looking for what others can't yet see in themselves – that untapped potential. He does this by looking for the spark and thinking about their pathway, rather than only seeing them through the lens of their current role.

What happens when a good hire doesn't work out?

Make the hard decisions on personnel early. No leader ever says, 'I wish I had taken longer to let people go', and yet it can be difficult to do.

There can be many different drivers for these people decisions. Often the person is good at their role, but maybe the company strategy has moved along, so it makes sense for that person to move on too, as a different skillset is required. It may be the organisation is shifting things globally or moving to a different location.

Equally, there may be individuals asking for too much money. They have had other bids in the market, which are attractive, and a start-up or scale-up simply can't compete with them.

In these moments, once the decision has been made, don't dance around it, delay or drag it out. Focus on the *how*, ie how do you plan to deliver the message? How will you communicate it? Put yourself in the shoes of the other person – how might they respond or react?

What emotions may come up? Preparation is key to ensuring the conversation goes as smoothly as possible.

Where you can, let the person you are letting go lead the messaging and cascade the news to their teams. There will be many things occupying their mind, from what people are saying to how their exit will impact their reputation. If they have a degree of control over the messaging, it will help.

If it is one of your senior people leaving and you are not the person communicating the decision, make sure to reach out to them directly. Offer to help them once they are willing to take help, which might be in the form of advice or introducing them to potentially interesting connections.

There are many times where leaders make the tough decisions (good person, wrong fit), yet the person leaves on amicable terms. Taking ownership of the decision rather than hiding is key. However, it is a different conversation entirely if the person is a jerk genius and toxic to the organisation (see Part Two: Applying The Learning).

Regularly evaluate your bench strength

As a company is scaling, different stages require different skills. Each year, Rick and his MarketAxess team do a skills inventory of their board, noting where they are as an organisation in accomplishing their long-term vision and where the skills gaps are.

For MSCI, Henry regularly asks himself, 'What holes in the human part of the company do we have that we need to close?' Agility and adaptability are key words stratospheric leaders shared throughout our conversations, which means making the necessary changes where needed. Evaluating your bench strength (board and leadership team) will determine whether you have the right people in the right seats.

It takes a good level of self-awareness to recognise your own strengths and weaknesses. You need a clear understanding of what the business needs, as well as your own skills gaps, and the confidence to hire the people who are potentially smarter than you or have the skills you don't. By doing this, you will bring the balance the business requires and have the people around you to make you a better leader. You need to hire these people to win and thrive.

The right people will encapsulate multiple components: intelligence quotient (IQ), emotional quotient (EQ), adversity quotient (AQ), which indicates a person's resilience and adaptability. It's also about you as the leader – what you value and what you perceive as lacking in yourself or in your core team.

Leading a business, after all, is a team sport and like all teams, you have specialist roles and need subject-matter experts. While leaders are 'inch experts' across their business, they will be looking to ensure the thresholds of expertise and mastery in each of the roles.

Also worthy of noting is that the word 'smart' can be a synonym for many attributes. Stratospheric leaders are looking for those around them to mirror the qualities of whatever smart means to them: work ethic, passion, energy, enthusiasm, courage, discipline, determination, drive. In other words, attributes that they feel are a baseline of success.

Plan for succession

Lance shares that for him, 'Every top-100 job in the firm needs to have at least one or two short-term successors and one or two longer-term ones.' There is a detailed plan, so if a person in a key role falls ill or leaves the organisation, there is somebody ready to step up quickly and take the reins.

In many organisations, rarely is the succession set-up clean, clear and tidy. Having a failsafe succession plan means being intentional as to who you are building and developing. Who could do each role if they were given a chance? How willing would they be to take over as the successor with an unknown timeframe? It also means as a leader being self-aware enough to have a good understanding of your longevity in the business. Leaders (especially founders) often find the second act hard.

Marshall Goldsmith's book *What Got You Here Won't Get You There* (Goldsmith, 2008) speaks of the importance of the *plan* and having an organised approach to bridge the development gaps, to nurture talents, to support future leaders in getting them to where you need them to be. You want the company to generate new leaders, ones who will be additive to the business.

When you leave your business, if you have done a good job as a leader, it will be in a stronger place. As Henry shares, 'I hope the day I announce my retirement, the stock price goes up 10%.' It doesn't mean you don't want to be missed, but you have the confidence you are leaving a strong team who won't miss a beat. Being an effective leader means building a long-term organisation that will endure – a company that isn't dependent on you.

Stratospheric leaders delegate

Once you have the right team around you, you (the leader) need to empower and give authority to others, allowing them to operate in their zones of genius. As Chris Willcox shares:

> 'You have a job as a leader to make decisions, but that doesn't mean executing every part of them. It's rarely the case that you need to decide how they get done. You need to figure out the things that you personally have

to be responsible for executing and what things you can delegate to the team around you.'

The last point Chris makes is incredibly motivating for the team too, ensuring people feel truly empowered. On a personal level, it can also be the thing that saves you from burnout.

Delegation requires you to be comfortable in your own skin and honest with the things you don't know or are not the expert on. It can be a little scary for leaders, as you are placing faith in others, which requires you to loosen the reins, but if you trust you have the right people, you have to trust them to act. Meddling, micromanaging, getting too involved in the details or being the control freak will inevitably disenfranchise and disempower them.

Lance shares:

> 'You have to let things that can be done by others be done by others. You don't have to do everything yourself. You need to have confidence that you have trained a person to do something well enough, and then be able to pass it on.'

This means striking the right balance between delegation and oversight.

In today's unpredictable world where everything is moving so fast, having a collegial management team offers a powerful coping mechanism, so decision making doesn't rest solely on your shoulders. This means having enough smart people on your team to provide input and feedback into the decisions you are making.

As Chris states, 'Any business that involves a one-man band is ultimately destined for some sort of disaster.' Unless, of course, it is in a time of crisis, where consensus may not be the right approach. In crisis events, you as leader may need to move from point A to point B in the shortest possible time for the business's survival. In these times, a more autocratic management style may be needed and can be the thing that saves you.

For all the leaders in the book, delegation is something that hasn't necessarily come naturally to them. Leaders can hire talented people, yet still find themselves making the decisions for them, because when you are obsessed with the direction of the company and the fine details, it's not easy to delegate and it can be uncomfortable letting others drive. You may also impose your own expectations, expecting others to be as fast or obsessive as you in getting things done.

As Henry shares:

> 'You have to resist the urge to be in the middle and you have to work really hard at it. Empower your people. Let them do what they need to do, trust that they know how, and then get out of their way.'

Be clear in your expectations

Growing a company is intrinsically linked to ambition, goals and aspirations, which inherently bring with them urgency and impatience. We all have our own unique way of seeing the world and as such, we associate different meanings with different words. If you want actions carried out urgently, for example, you have to explain what you mean *specifically* and ensure an alignment of understanding. Does urgent mean following up on a client request within an hour or in two to three days?

Create a shared cultural understanding of terminology around the things that matter to you such as urgency, responsiveness of following up, etc. It will give you the trust you need to be able to step back.

For many of our stratospheric leaders, it is not a question of whether to delegate or not. They are passionate about their businesses and have intellectual curiosity, but they don't want to be involved in everything. They simply want to know what is going on.

How do you strike the right balance between being close to the business while not getting too involved? This means making sure the right information flow comes to you. Be clear to others on what is relevant to you. What do you want to monitor closely? How often do you want to be updated?

Put in place mechanisms by which you are informed. At MSCI, an email is sent out every time the business completes a sale of more than $50,000. It includes a description, a paragraph on what motivated the client to subscribe to the product, and it gives credit to the people who helped get the deal done. It's an example of a way Henry keeps himself informed rather than regularly calling people asking, 'How's it going?'

Henry shares, 'There is not one single path to success.' For some leaders, the only way to get something done is the way they would do it. This doesn't mean never giving advice, but it does require a level of self-awareness to recognise where you are imparting your way and potentially stifling the creativity in others. There is a distinct difference between, 'Call the client back and tell them the following' and 'If I were doing this, this is what I would do, but you need to figure out the path that feels right to you'.

Your people first, and then the customer

For some businesses, the rule is to put the customer first, and then everything else will follow. However, when it comes to relationships, inspirational speaker and author Simon Sinek makes a valid point: 'Customers will never love a company until the employees love it first' (Sinek, 2014). Your business can take a customer-centric view, but it'll be your people who facilitate those relationships, who convey your message and cultivate your reputation. It's all about your people, hence the importance of intentionality around hiring a world-class team with cultural fit, and not just hiring for competence and capability.

It is important as a leader to be accessible to your people, but this requires balance and managing. As the business scales and you empower those around you, you need to allow them to be in their roles and reinforce the institutional recognition and respect that comes with their job title. You can't be as accessible to everyone in the organisation in the same way as you were before.

Most leaders would recognise and understand the above to be true, yet often they allow people in the organisation to circumnavigate their line manager, coming directly to the person at the top – a term known as 'skip-levelling'. When this is done badly, the hierarchy is effectively broken, which can lead to a negative spiral of frustration, mistrust and uncertainty for the leader who has been bypassed.

This isn't to say skip-levelling should never happen. It is valuable for leaders to hear different voices from different parts of the business, but it requires openness and transparency. For example, you as the leader need to ensure you are OK to share with the person skip-levelled whatever you discussed with their direct report.

When you're a leader, skip-levelling is something to be mindful of. Many people will be competing for your time and attention. The structure and rules of engagement you put in place are critical and will strongly influence motivation and morale. Leaders set the tone, so it is always important to be conscious as to what you are role-modelling.

Motivating those around you

Emotions can ripple out and magnify rapidly. Given leaders set the tone, the emotion you bring to a meeting – how you walk into a room – matters.

Lance speaks of the importance of positivity: 'Being positive is infectious. It fuels you and others.' I am sure we have all had experiences with an 'energy vampire', the person who sucks every ounce of creativity and life out of the room; the person who changes the course of a conversation negatively. There is a ripple of impact and it is an undesirable one.

If you want positivity, passion and enthusiasm to radiate out, you as a leader must bring these attributes. It's a real leadership skill to stay positive, so it needs to be practised. Attitudes are contagious, and it is important that you demonstrate those that are worth catching.

Lance shares one of the things he likes to do is lead by example. 'I've never been the general in the headquarters calling out the orders. I'd rather be the general in the field with the troops.' For him, this translates as making calls to clients (especially when there is an issue), being in the room developing the products, working up the strategy and the execution plans, participating and engaging from the front rather than approving and directing from the back.

All the leaders in the book are 'in the field' types. This, however, means considering how much you are in the trenches and making sure it's not micromanagement. It's a careful but essential balance to strike.

Although it can be difficult in large organisations to know everybody, where you can, make a concerted effort to remember and use a person's name. Being addressed by name impacts people physiologically, so it can be a real motivational boost when somebody senior acknowledges them in this way. It shows you value them, and builds connection and rapport, a basis for any level of trust.

Listen to your teams

Growing a business or leading teams in today's world of heightened disruption invariably means long, demanding hours, intensity, pressure and stress. How will you know if you are pushing them too hard?

It all starts with awareness, which means really knowing your people. There are always clues to overwhelm, whether it's irritability, impatience, somebody being more emotionally triggered than usual, looking exhausted. Listen to their tone of voice (ie the body language of the voice). Be intentional in looking out for these signs and understand that people have different capacities, so you need to know what each person can cope with. Your capacity doesn't equal theirs.

Ask that your team members openly share with you if they find themselves getting stuck in survival mode – that highly overwhelming, fraught and anxious place – and you have to genuinely mean it. As a leader, you don't know what you don't know (you are not a mind reader) and you can only act on the information available to you, hence an agreement of openness with your people is essential. Human beings can do a great job of having the corporate mask firmly welded on, appearing calm and controlled on the outside. Nobody sees the lagoon of anxiety, worry and fear a person may be experiencing on the inside.

If you as a leader have created a high trust space, you can openly share what you are observing in a person's behaviour and actions, to catch overwhelm and to support them before they find themselves entering the place of diminishing returns. Open dialogue is key, while being mindful not to have this conversation publicly or corner a person.

It is worth giving people real influence (or perceived influence over the direction and the evolution of the organisation – a voice that is truly heard, if not a vote). When they feel they are part of the business's process, you will typically get more human power. It becomes harder for people to question or complain about the workload when they are effectively instigating it. Because group consensus for decision making requires more open dialogue, you will also get the transparency as to where somebody is energy-wise for free on the way.

Lastly, ask your team members, 'How will I know if you are being pushed too far? What will I notice in your actions, behaviours?' Getting the most positive yield out of your people in a human-centred way that is good for them requires an investment of your attention. This is never a one-and-done conversation, but an ongoing dialogue. Responsibility for maintaining this dialogue sits with the leader.

Make mistakes, but learn from them

In the entrepreneurial space, you want people to bring their creative and courageous mindset. To enable that, you need to ensure they have the confidence to share their ideas and decisions, comfortable in the knowledge they may not work out. You want people to take chances, which means helping them recognise that mistakes are part of the learning journey, encouraging them not to blame or point the finger, but to stand up and take responsibility. Sometimes, you need to reward people for making the call, even if the call doesn't work.

Lance talks about the importance of getting behind people – because you won't get to where you are going if you don't make a few mistakes. As he shares, 'You don't become Lewis Hamilton if you haven't crashed a few cars.' One mistake does not mean failure or defeat.

Make the mistakes, but learn from them, even the somewhat punitive ones. In the culture of entrepreneurship, people realise that you cannot be right all the time. Mistakes and wrong decisions are part of the process of pushing the envelope in what can be done better. Listen to and respect all your people's decisions and, importantly, the learnings they take from the wrong ones.

Don't be the chatterbox

Early in Lance's career, he was told, 'Two ears, one mouth. Listen twice as much as you speak', and he credits this as being one of the best pieces of advice he ever received. He candidly shares that he didn't actually take the advice properly until he was in his late forties, perfecting the talent in his fifties.

It is so easy to underestimate the importance of listening. In my experience, a lot of high-performance leaders are so excited about getting the decision moving faster, they find themselves, literally and figuratively, finishing others' sentences. They are thinking ahead and as a result, they are missing a whole bunch of valuable information.

Listening is an active behaviour, not a passive response, yet so often, a leader's body language gives away the signs that they are not fully engaged. They are distracted, looking at their digital devices, preoccupied in their thinking.

The quality of your listening will determine the quality of the other person's thinking. Your non-verbals demonstrate if you are really listening, so are a force of encouragement or discouragement. If you look bored, the person you are listening to will be boring. If you fidget, they will rush. If you seem angry, they will tiptoe.

Listen and *silent* have the same letters. Listening means giving space for others to speak and having the quality of attention that shows you are engaged, for example leaning in or holding eye contact. These are all signals that you're listening and you are doing it with respect. As Lance says, 'It's a sign of good manners.'

The space afforded by listening offers valuable time for reflection, understanding and processing of information. It allows you to notice the entire person – not only the words, but also the sentiment behind them. It generates fresh insights and helps you learn what people really care about.

As Lee shared, listening means knowing what part you play in the conversation. Are you there to share information as part of your agenda or are you there to listen to your team and their agenda? The latter is a worthy point to underscore. When the leader speaks first, knowingly or unknowingly, others will adopt their opinion or perspective. It can limit the ideas and thoughts they share, so it is important as a leader to know your role. In which meetings is it best for you to speak last?

Understand people

A powerful quality observed in stratospheric leaders linked to their listening is curiosity – showing a real and genuine interest in another person. When it comes to personal relationships, we tend to get back what we put in, and the same applies to our work relationships. Leaders are in the business of people and a way to achieve high-quality connection with another person is through showing authentic interest in them. Yet, rarely is this executed well.

When it is faked, ie you ask a question because you feel you *should* or *have to*, people feel the negative energy behind it. Buddhists speak of approaching situations with a beginner's mind, and yet many of us do the opposite.

A way to show interest could simply be to do your research ahead of meeting somebody. For new connections, so much information is available on the internet, easily enabling you to get a sense of who the person is, their interests, what boards they may sit on, notable moments in their career. It means you can identify any commonalities and themes to discuss, and plan interesting questions or conversation starters.

Henry affirms the importance of research ahead of meeting someone. In his words, 'preparation in advance influences a different outcome'. A meeting or engagement can look impromptu, but Henry will have done his homework. He thinks about ways to connect to make the other person feel good, saying, 'The most consequential thing is how you have made somebody feel at the end of your time together. It is incredibly powerful.'

Lance shared a story about an interview with David Solomon (CEO of Goldman Sachs). Ahead of the meeting, his research showed that one of David's hobbies was to DJ garage music, so towards the end of the interview, he asked, 'House or garage?'

It is widely known that David Solomon enjoys DJing, and so one could assume Lance's question was based on generic information about him, but it was all about the way he asked the question, digging deeper (Lance had researched the difference between house and garage). This showed connection at an elevated level.

How you show up matters. Preparation is king. It is a great way to build valuable connective tissue with another person, but it's often the forgotten child. When we look at the difference that makes a difference, it is often the small things that many overlook or underestimate the value of.

As Lance notes, if you are travelling on a work trip to India, don't be the person who says, 'I hate cricket.' Even if it is a sport you are not fond of, instead say, 'I'd love to know more about your national game.'

Shane Akeroyd (former IHS Markit executive) speaks of the importance of observing cues from the environment. You have a choice at the start of a meeting: you can go straight to the agenda, or you can ask a question, maybe commenting on the artwork on the wall, the family pictures on the desk, the history books on the shelf, the baseball mementos displayed. Tuning into the environment gives you valuable clues to a person's interests and hobbies, and it offers a great platform for a question to build connection.

Give thought now to a time when somebody asked you a question about yourself and they were genuinely interested in what you had to say, which presented itself in how they listened. They actively demonstrated they had done their homework ahead of meeting you. How did it make you feel? Chances are it felt pretty good. It is always good to feel seen and heard, no matter who you are.

As Dale Carnegie said, 'You can make more friends in two months by becoming interested in other people than you can in two years by trying to get other people interested in you' (Carnegie, 2012). Relationships are built on the ability to listen, react and understand; to be interested. A leader who asks questions and remembers the answers, who remembers when a colleague has been under the weather or has a poorly relative, is a leader who makes an emotional connection and builds trust.

Part of being interested is being interesting – having an opinion, telling stories and sharing insights. Lance says:

'You have to be interesting at a level that is above most, because you're going to need people around you. People are going to respond to you based on your personality. Also your manners and the way you deal with people matter. They will influence the quality of your connections.'

To be interesting, you need to know what's going on, whether that's through reading, listening or observing. The stratospheric leaders I interviewed for this book are always tuned in, curious, learning and have a perspective or something to contribute. As a result, when our conversations did meander (discussions on the Big Green Egg barbecue, fairtrade coffee, the band Nickelback, air gliders), they always had some fun insight to bring.

The people we spend time with influence us more than we may realise. If you surround yourself with interesting and interested people, you are going to develop a workplace that people will aspire to be a part of.

Crucial conversations

As you ascend, lead more people, have greater responsibility and more decision-making power, you will be required to have the high-value, high-stake crucial conversations relating to topics such as giving feedback, letting somebody go, addressing allegations, pay reviews, organisational structure changes etc. It is important to stress the word *crucial*, because these conversations can often be referred to as 'difficult' or 'uncomfortable', and our choice of words matters. Words invoke emotions and using ones such as 'difficult' can create fear before the conversation even starts. Likewise, seeing these conversations as uncomfortable can lead to avoidance. We just don't want to deal with the discomfort of the meeting or its potential fallout.

None of our stratospheric CEOs have professed to love these types of discussions, but they have put strategies in place to do them well. Avoidance rarely serves either party. It simply defers and often accentuates the problem.

To do crucial conversations well, you start with preparation. Before a match, a sports team will train. Before a concert, a musician rehearses. Preparation for crucial conversations can happen in much the same way.

It starts with you holding the mirror up and asking yourself, 'What emotional baggage might I be bringing into this conversation? What happened? What stories might I be telling myself about the other person/people? What assumptions might I be making?' Then give thought to what you are sharing, asking yourself, 'How might the other person/people receive it? What might they know that I don't? What other perspectives might there be?'

Once you are in the conversation, the key thing is to stick to the facts and not bring in your own interpretations. As Rick shares:

> 'Be forthright and clear that there is no other agenda aside from what you are telling them. Be honest with what the conversation is about. Don't ameliorate the message. Put it in a way that is understandable, simple, direct and empathetic.'

Put yourself in the other person's shoes and pre-empt what their reaction may be. Preparation enables you to practise the inevitable discomfort, getting comfortable with the uncomfortable.

Give thought to the top ten questions that may come up in the conversation, and then identify the terrible three. These are the three questions that you would really prefer not to be asked. It's similar to a military approach – anticipating what may be coming. Should the terrible three questions be asked, you will feel bulletproof inside if you have already given thought to a response.

Active listening, which is done by making eye contact and asking questions with genuine interest in the response, will demonstrate empathy and respect. Give thought to your desired outcome of the conversation. Winning at all costs won't benefit you long term, so what could make it a win-win?

Finally, during critical conversations, do check in on your emotional state. When emotion runs high, intellect runs low. Recognise when a pause or slowing down would benefit everyone involved and the goal of the meeting.

Receiving feedback

One area that's often considered a challenging conversation is giving and receiving feedback, yet when it's executed in the right way, it is a gift and a valuable learning opportunity. After all, we don't know what we don't know, and we all have developmental areas and room for improvement.

When you are at the apex of an organisation, you are putting yourself out there. Many people will have a view on you and will feel licensed to comment on you personally. Leadership can be challenging as you have a diverse audience with diverse views, and as a result, there can be a huge variance in the comments you receive, some of which will be diametrically opposed, so how do you best approach feedback?

Chris highlights the importance of being rational and not taking things too personally. Look at the balance between these things. There will be good feedback and negative comments, and it's important not to spend too much time on the isolated pieces of personal criticism:

'If feedback is real and not a personal bias, it won't be one piece of feedback, but multiple comments along the same lines. You will see patterns. There is something there and it's not somebody just having a bad day. Observing the themes highlights what needs your attention. Pay attention to patterns.'

The balance is having a thick enough skin to be OK with criticism, while not growing such a thick skin you don't listen to anything anybody says. Recognising which voices matter, and then listening to them, will offer you valuable data points for your growth.

Although it can be tough to receive the negative comments, Henry reminds himself to keep an open mind and that an ignorance of his blind spots is a worse option. To receive feedback means asking for it and really meaning it. The article '9 New Year's resolutions for leaders in 2024' (Forbes, 2023) recommends we ask others what our bad boss traits are. It is easy to be well intentioned and still get things wrong.

As a leader, you will often receive the polished apple, as people may be too afraid to share critical feedback, or they won't see any upside. The longer this goes on, the riskier it becomes for a leader. Chris says it's your job to create the safe space where people feel they can openly share and disclose without any fear of retribution or negative impact.

Without feedback, you will find yourself in a vacuum, and even if you do a great job of self-appraisal, evaluating the interactions you have had and the decisions you have made, rarely is this entirely objective and there will be gaps. That said, regular self-evaluation should mean feedback becomes easier to receive and hopefully any criticism is less of a surprise.

Lee advises you to ask yourself, 'What perceptions do people have of me? What can I learn from their feedback?'

What about you giving feedback as a leader? The single biggest skill gap for many leaders is telling people the truth about their performance and their shortcomings. It is the gift that is rarely given. As the execution of this feedback strongly determines how you will make the person receiving it feel, what do you need to be mindful of?

Rick says it's about speaking to the person concerning their behaviour and its effect on you and the team while not personalising the feedback or adding your own interpretation, commentary or judgement. Keep your observation short and to the point. Invite a response early in the conversation, so it becomes a two-way dialogue rather than a monologue.

For Lance, it's about giving the tough messages when they are needed and approaching them with transparency and honesty. As my friend Laurie Aaron says, candid vs candy-coated. It's a discussion and Lance invites the other person to go first. He shares:

> 'Let's say for example the feedback is around executive presence. I might say, "Tell me how you think your meeting presence was in that last meeting. What are one or two things you can do to improve on that?" Then when they have responded, I say, "You know what, I really liked those points you made and I want to help you do better."'

In organisational psychologist Adam Grant's book, *Hidden Potential* (Grant, 2023), he talks about the nineteen words to use that will fundamentally shift how receptive a person is to comments you share: 'I am giving you these comments because I have very high expectations and I'm confident you can reach them.' People typically have a knee-jerk reaction to the word 'feedback' and it's not a positive one. Sharing your positive intent and substituting the word 'comments' for 'feedback' is likely to have a far better outcome for both sides.

Managing differences of opinion

As Rick shares, 'It's OK to disagree, just don't be disagreeable.' Difference of opinion should be welcome. After all, you want the constructive contrarians and those who bring an alternative lens and way of seeing a situation or problem.

Chris also references the importance of recognising perspective. There is no single truth about a person or a business. Everyone has a different lens and sees things in a different way. Sometimes these lenses can come into or out of focus and some may become more important than others. It is the job of the leader to ensure that every lens is represented, because no one view is complete without the others.

This is where the curiosity muscle comes in. You can equally be right and wrong in a situation. Asking incisive questions will broaden your perspective.

Summary

Stratospheric leaders are smart, savvy and know themselves and their markets well. Their decisions are reflective of their ambition and their vision.

They recognise that to be highly successful, you as a leader have to be intentional about your people, knowing their skills and their talents. This means developing a leadership team that supplements your own skills and supports and mitigates your blind spots.

Stratospheric leaders invest time in building relationships, bringing curiosity to understand how their people think, while assessing their skills, areas of focus and talents. Being interested not only gains you valuable knowledge, it also creates enshrined trust in the relationship, and as a result people generally respect what is being communicated, because they understand the intent and that the decision is in service to the business. This is especially important when it comes to people management.

In the business world, it is often the big egos that are held up in high esteem. The leaders profiled in this book show ego isn't the only way. The human side of leadership, being people focused, is a powerful recipe for innovation and success. The nicest and most empathetic of leaders are in my experience also the most ruthless, driven, focused and determined. These are positive traits in the right context. Stratospheric leaders are strategic operators and that's a good thing. It is in part what has made their organisations stronger and more successful than most.

SIX

Culture And Values

'A strong culture is the greatest asset a
company can cultivate.'

Lance Uggla

To be the company of the future means creating an organisation people want to be part of. As Chris Willcox says, it needs to be 'one that your people are excited to belong to'.

A company has a culture whether it is intentional or not. People can 'read' the culture from signs such as the vocabulary used to what gets prioritised and who gets promoted. The best and most successful companies have a culture that is deliberate and constantly evolving. It is the foundation upon which a company's strategy is built. When you get culture right, it brings with it a huge competitive advantage and fosters the results the company is looking to deliver.

Stratospheric leaders understand that everybody in a company plays a vital part in creating and perpetuating its culture, but what specifically *is* culture? It transcends the superficial, going beyond a logo or a list of impressive-looking nouns such as integrity, trust, customer focus, excellence emblazoned on the company website. A great visual brand and some invigorating corporate prose should reflect it, but ultimately your culture is woven by your people. The way they walk, talk and behave; the way they go about their work, and the individual and collective values they live by. These are behaviours that can be scaled and drive mission-critical results.

The strongest of organisations have clear values reflecting what is meaningful to them. With values, an immense chasm can exist between founder-led businesses and those where the CEO changes every three to five years, which has become the reality for many Fortune 500 and FTSE 100 companies. These organisations may have beautifully crafted mission statements and invest heavily in defining their core values, yet the executives fail to embody and propagate them or even seem to understand them. There is no trickle down or absorption, just a bunch of nice words.

Act on what you say

This is the case for the stratospheric leader. Their entire organisation operates on a bedrock of unwavering principles – ones that are not just words, but living and breathing standards, equally conscious and intentional, and unconscious and instinctive. These standards are measured and individuals held to account.

Culture starts at the top. It is how you turn up as leader and what you do day after day. Your behaviours represent you. Leaders set the tone and there are no exceptions. Deliver on your promises and be consistent with your execution. Behaviours such as attention to detail, preparation, effort, being on time for meetings show an attitude of respect and are values that should come easily.

Creating culture and then enabling its percolation takes effort. Even unconscious culture has been honed and is preserved through its continuation. The 'lived values' require an investment of time with even greater effort and focus to measure culture results and the accountability in relation to them.

Stratospheric leaders understand the right cultural tone creates a huge advantage, serving to attract and retain the best people. It makes your organisation a 'destination' employer for top talent and brings pride in the brand and a sense of belonging. Getting culture right isn't a nice to have, it's critical in creating a world-leading and enduring business.

If you are being honest with yourself, are your company values the lived and breathed experience of your stakeholders? How consistent are you in what you say and what you do? How does the statement on the wall translate into practice? For instance, are the values part of the performance-management processes? Do they impact who gets promoted, who is asked to leave the organisation?

Lance Uggla built IHS Markit with a foundation of unwavering principles: accountability, innovation, integrity and, most notably, partnership. These words are deeply thought through. Partnership is critical for him, the company mission being a collective endeavour. He wants his leaders to feel a sense of ownership and to lead the firm together.

This saw him create a partnership model of forty leaders from across the firm, who would share a pool of an additional financial incentive. Perhaps surprisingly, the performance of this group was not measured by the traditional financial metrics of success such as profit, sales, revenue, earnings before interest, taxes, depreciation and amortisation (EBITDA) or earnings per share (EPS). This was both unique and innovative, and meant that there was an immediate focus on broader accomplishment.

The IHS Markit partnership was measured by soft skills: non-commercial activities such as involvement in the intern programme, mentorship, taking charitable days with the team, partnering in recruitment, being an inclusive leader and reading what's going on in the office. Lance wanted his leaders to participate in aspects of the broader organisation that did not directly or immediately benefit themselves, but created connectivity, communication and camaraderie across teams. He felt that this type of accessibility and humanising of leaders mitigated the inevitable corporate hierarchy and helped to reduce politicking. Dismantling hierarchy, even in small, short bursts, allows connections to be developed with the ability to have new direct relationships that criss-cross an organisation.

For Lance, every partner was expected to play a key part in growing the company culture. He wanted his people to be the culture, embody it and to have pride in the brand. 'Win together and struggle through together' was the motto. He made the journey enjoyable – intentionally and purposely. Although his team would say his style never felt forced, it was honed, refined and deliberate. He showed up to every meeting like he wouldn't want to be anywhere else – his attitude and his actions set the tone.

For Henry Fernandez, partnership and fairness were key in perpetuating the culture he wanted to develop. His culture was one based on capability, contribution and achievement. From the start, he focused on how compensation could correlate to the behaviours and actions he regarded as critical. His focus was to build a non-politicised organisation with cohesive and collaborative teams, not fiefdoms that battled for internal resources or recognition. This meant clear focus on impact and contribution (which was measured on multiple frameworks), a balanced meritocracy with a continual focus on the institution, the organism of the company, not individuals or bosses.

Collaboration creates collective cultures

Chris argues that building and maintaining culture must be shared by everybody who walks into the building. It's about all the people. Lance likens this kind of collaboration to the wonderful Kenyan proverb, 'sticks in a bundle are unbreakable'. For him, it is the team over the individual and the partnership serving to inspire each partner. Collaboration offers clarity on the expectations of each other and creates an environment and culture of togetherness.

Lance wanted to see passion in the partnership he created in his business, and for him passion is more than just demonstrating excitement. He expected his team to be organised in their thoughts and strategies, which they could recommend with true enthusiasm. Without a clear, organised and prepared strategy, he says, it is difficult to feel the passion behind any business plan.

Positivity, passion, respect, manners, integrity, innovation; IHS Markit's values all began with Lance. These words translated into real behaviour – modelling what he wanted emulated and being consistent and insistent, Lance set the high standard and expected others to follow. No exceptions.

The MarketAxess culture is cohesive and clear and embodies Rick McVey's deep-rooted core values of collaboration, imagination, inclusivity, agility and tenacity. 'If you are not taking advantage of the input around you,' he says, 'you are making an enormous mistake.'

Collaboration plays out in the flat organisational structure, and Rick actively welcomes opinions and encourages people to express their views and input into key decisions. This is critical when you are seeking to transform and disrupt. The best insights can come from anywhere in the organisation. Rick knows the monopoly of the best ideas does not lie with him and will admit he doesn't have all the answers. Inclusive and open environments provide valuable checkpoints, which Rick says layer confidence when you're making the tough decisions and, more often than not, drive a better conclusion.

Chris shares, 'As a leader, it is important to let go of any self-imposed expectations to have all the answers. A big part of being a leader is bringing other people into the problem solving.'

Integrity and transparency are foundations of a trust culture

Inclusive environments build trust, which is the lifeblood of any organisation, but there are layers to trust. It firstly needs to be latticed across and within teams, which then builds the institutional trust.

Chris notes that without trust, you don't have a long-term sustainable business in any field. In the absence of deep and enduring trust, culture will be built on sand, lasting only as long as the first strong wind or high tide. On the flip side, a healthy organisation with deep-seated belief in its roots can withstand the inevitable crises of the modern-day world, where unpredictability and uncertainty are inevitable. Its trust culture allows people to push and challenge each other to find new innovative ways to realise the shared organisational goals.

An inclusive culture of trust requires transparency. Rick speaks of transparency being equity, which ultimately engenders trust and loyalty. Transparency also avoids people second-guessing you or leaning into stories that are simply not backed by fact.

Henry agrees: 'The more you can create an open culture, the less watercooler secrets there are.' These conversations are rarely healthy, most loaded with assumptions and opinions presented as facts.

Henry has ensured that every stage of MSCI's journey has been driven by clarity and transparency. One core facet of this is that complex ideas are not pursued until they can be described simply. This means decisions will rarely be misunderstood or actioned for what could be the wrong reasons.

Furthermore, the MSCI culture is one where people are expected to be direct, but polite, constructive and collegial. Anyone in the organisation is entitled to go anywhere and talk to anybody. Everyone can have an opinion, but bad behaviour is not tolerated.

This culture treads a fine line that allows questioning, but not the concept of blame or mistrust. Questions, although direct, are not permitted to be accusatory. Active debate and challenge are encouraged, but with appropriate tones and structure. Although this can be a tough culture to manage and may not work for all organisations, it defines MSCI and is one that has enabled a strong community and camaraderie in its organisation.

If you have the right teams around you with the right skillsets, they generally get to the bottom of any problem. Build the right culture and success will come.

Transparency extends across clients and customers. Michael Spencer speaks of clients always coming first in every strategic and tactical decision being made to enhance their experience, while Lance talks about not rolling out new policies until you have spoken to everyone impacted by them. You don't raise prices, for example, without speaking to your customers and explaining why. Sometimes this won't initially appear to be the most profitable approach and sometimes it means you won't be fastest to the market, but you will know you have operated with integrity and that will always pay dividends in the long run.

Team members who trust each other are more likely to be comfortable being open, owning their failures, weaknesses and fears. Many leaders believe they need to have the corporate mask firmly welded on and hide any form of vulnerability. In part this is true – your people will look at you and they want to see leadership qualities of confidence, certainty and conviction. At the same time, they want to get a sense of who their leader is when you are not in your seat – to see and experience the human side.

When Lance was diagnosed with prostate cancer, he chose to open up about it and share his diagnosis with the organisation. Principally, he did this to raise awareness of the disease, but it also demonstrated that no one is infallible. His courage and humanity brought him even closer to his people.

There is power in openness. It creates bonds.

Accessible leadership and active, honest communication

A key component of trust is the human connection. When you ask Lance's senior team members how he leads, they describe him as being highly personable, honest and visible, building connections at all levels of the organisation and the business.

A big ask of leaders in today's world is that they are personable, which is great for those to whom it comes naturally. For those who find it more challenging, I advise them to be accessible. That is a behaviour that can be managed, and it does build trust. The more you know about somebody, the more you can trust them.

Accessibility includes active, honest communication styles. Chris speaks of the importance of a culture underpinned by telling the truth in your speeches and in your town halls. Every engagement is an opportunity to reinforce the company values and you as leader are the chief repetition officer. Being clear and honest about the shortcomings of the business and industry is necessary, even if it is uncomfortable. Your people will appreciate being informed on how decisions are made.

This means creating a culture where it is OK for everyone to speak the uncomfortable truths without fear of retribution. The most junior person should feel they can challenge the most senior people as long as they have evidence-based data. It's not about the hippos – the highest-paid person's opinions. As human beings, we are not typically truth seeking in nature, as truths can be uncomfortable, awkward, feel confrontational, make people defensive, which is why we tend to avoid them. To counteract this means having a culture that is open to many opinions and having the mechanisms in place to enable this.

Part of being a trusted leader means informing your people when important events happen. It may be a member of your executive committee announcing they are leaving, a decision to retrench or the closing down of a business or product. In these situations, Henry will call every single member of the executive committee together to break the news, to share what is coming. He doesn't do it via email or group meetings.

Why is his approach important? Henry wants his leadership team members to know if there is a problem, good news, bad news, they will hear it immediately (or as immediately as is reasonable) from him and not a third party. This gives people the opportunity to ask questions in real time, which as a leader he can respond to in real time. It also relaxes people. They know they don't have to be working the rumour mill to get their information.

With this kind of honest communication, people are less likely to think you are withholding information from them, with some in the know and others not, which can destroy culture. As a leader, you tread a fine balance between what you can disclose and what you may not/cannot/should not reveal. With an open and honest culture, the people around you will be accepting of that. They won't, however, accept crucial information being hidden from them or feeling they have been misled.

Remember, always conveying positivity isn't authentic or real. People value being informed, even if it isn't always the message they want to hear. By communicating the challenges, you are inviting your people to help you change things – collectively, collaboratively, consciously. This allows you to see who is looking to work towards a solution and who is faking it (which people can see through).

Vulnerability and emotions are contagious. Much like microbes, they will quickly ripple through an organisation in your words, behaviours, actions and in your non-verbals – the silent messaging. However, this can be a narrow tightrope to walk. People want their leaders to be confident, clear and calm, but they also want them to be human – especially in times of crisis.

Ask yourself what behavioural qualities you need to bring to a situation/event/meeting to achieve the desired outcome. Use this insight to inform how you show up and the type of energy you are bringing with you. For instance, a leader can share that there is a serious concern people need to know about, while at the same time outlining a plan to overcome it. In this way, the contagious emotion they convey is realistic optimism and not 'Oh my God, everything is on fire!' Incidentally, the latter is an effective way to lose great people. People stick around when they believe the future is positive and leave when they see a train wreck coming.

Perpetuating a culture – hire for fit

Once you have established the business's culture and are living it, you need to hire people to fit. Stratospheric leaders recognise that culture is a living organism. They want to ensure the inputs (their people) preserve the culture's authenticity, which can be one of the hardest things to do.

Henry teaches us that organisations need to establish an honest and open culture from day one, building it from the ground up. This means thinking about new hires and intentionally creating the team you need to support and enhance your culture. Hiring must be based on competence and cultural fit, but all too often the latter becomes the forgotten child. If you focus solely on performance and skillset in isolation, how do you protect the culture you have worked hard to create?

When Henry is hiring, evidence of teamwork trumps all else. He is looking for culture carriers in every candidate. These are people who care about all aspects of the chain – those who are willing to pitch in and are humble. In the interview process, he examines language; he listens for 'we' versus 'I'. He seeks to understand how self-aware a candidate is or, conversely, how much of an ego they bring.

For example, does a candidate personalise their successes? Can they evidence bringing in the opinions of others and teamwork? Can they speak thoughtfully of their strengths, weaknesses and developmental areas? Can they speak of the perceived versus the actual? Sometimes, showing a weakness is a strength. It demonstrates a high order level of thinking, which is a rare quality.

Henry refers to the interview as an X-ray of the individual. Who are they on the inside? How do they think? How do they process information? He is putting himself in their head, seeking to understand what makes them turn left or right in a decision.

He also regards the interview as an invitation for the candidate to do an X-ray on the company. A symbiotic fit is essential. He prepares diligently ahead of any interview, reading the CV several times and taking notes, so in the interview itself, he doesn't want the candidate to walk him through it. Instead, he wants them to evidence *how* they achieved the results and the skills they used, and as the interviewee responds to his questions, he is closely observing how they explain, adapt, react. One of his key questions (which I love) is 'How do you create happiness in your job?'

Lee Olesky shares the importance of making the right hires early in the life of an organisation – individuals with shared ethics, values and attitudes – because it establishes your culture from the start. It then perpetuates and your first hires create a standard for the rest to follow.

Leaders usually replicate themselves in their own hiring, so if the CEO hires a leader who does not have great cultural fit, over time, everyone *they* hire will share the same characteristics. Soon, you have an entire division full of leaders, middle managers and first-level managers who don't role model the desired culture. If you don't get it right at the beginning, it is difficult to change the culture later.

One organisation I have worked with has an interview guide that is placed in the hands of all hiring managers. It outlines sample questions to ask candidates and questions that should *never* be asked. The book includes a set of values-based questions. For instance, if ownership is a value, among the interview questions might be, 'Tell me about a time in your career when you acted as an owner of an important project. What did you do and not do?' It helps greatly when company values are phrased as action, for example, 'Act as an owner', 'Lead with integrity', bringing with it transparency and clarity on what is measured.

Consider your own hiring process. Do you have qualitative and quantitative measures in it and are these systemised? How does hiring for culture and character feed into your process?

The culture at MSCI is so embedded and well communicated that everyone involved in the hiring process is focused on a candidate's match for values. They know how important this is. Henry is very clear MSCI does not hire jerks. His leaders hire team players.

At MSCI, it is OK to hire somebody who will speak their mind. It's not OK to hire people who put their interests and success ahead of the team's, ie those individuals who will destroy the company culture. Henry will not hire people who could be cancerous, and on the rare occasion those people do get hired, he finds they typically part ways within a year because their behaviour is not tolerated.

Henry believes many people confuse the egotistical, arrogant prima donna with someone who may not be easy to manage or get along with. 'Rock stars' – the A+ players – are great to have on the team as they will drive the evolution of the business and attract other A+ players, but they must be part of the 'band', much like Mick Jagger, for all his ego, is part of the Rolling Stones. If you can combine the talent and the ego to create an incredible group, you will have a hit on your hands.

A company's culture will always be defined by its worst-tolerated behaviour

All the CEOs included in the book agree bad behaviour will never be tolerated, but there is a difference between general bad behaviour that all companies experience and the bad behaviour that is at odds with the company culture. They recognise that any form of bad behaviour will contaminate and corrode the culture, but if you are allowing people to be living contradictions of the company values, it will lead others to question you as a leader. There is no room for the jerk genius even if you build a big moat around them. If you have a jerk non-genius on the team, that's a different problem altogether.

Stratospheric leaders are focused on ensuring their organisation's culture is maintained. They are willing to hire and, more importantly, fire based on the company's core values. Look at the qualities and behaviours of the people in your business: does each person exemplify the culture or undermine it?

Ongoing culture cultivation

In pursuit of continuous improvement, Rick asked Mary Sedarat, MarketAxess Chief People Officer, to pick a group of positive culture carriers from across the organisation: individuals who embody the company values. These people now have an open communication channel to the leadership team, to share how they feel MarketAxess can be doing better and how it can improve. Change at MarketAxess is embraced.

The best way to assess culture is to really listen to how your employees are describing the organisation and the environment. They will see things that you don't. The invisible becomes visible, and it gives you the ability to act on an issue before it becomes a bigger problem. Feedback is rarely eternal judgement and there will always be a seed of learning.

Once new individuals are hired into an organisation, it is important they too feel they can contribute to the ongoing process of culture cultivation. Stratospheric CEOs are intentional about developing systematic ways of inculcating the organisations' values, such as creating culture committees, appointing culture champions, taking soundings, running polls, carrying out employee engagement surveys and finding ways to acknowledge those who go above and beyond. Rewarding those individuals whose behaviours personify the values of the organisation will deliver a powerful message.

Similarly, regular conversations with your most innovative thinkers will ensure you are not simply agreeing a nice set of platitudes.

Instead, your values accurately reflect where you all are as an organisation and, equally importantly, where you are heading to. Values are words that need to be symbolic of your organisation's lived culture, otherwise they will have no more influence than changing the colour of your logo.

I have a 'friend-tor' – Mark Beeston, founder of Illuminate Financial – who has been one of the key people I have bounced ideas off in creating this book. When it comes to clients and culture, he speaks of Illuminate's success being built on long-term relationships and maintaining those relationships. In fact, often his people built relationships when they had nothing to sell at that moment.

Illuminate adopted karma as a core value, helping people along the way, which in turn has opened up new opportunities and networks. He intentionally misquoted the classic wisdom, supposedly from pioneer of marketing John Wanamaker (B2B Marketing, 2015) around advertising spend, saying, 'Half of my time meeting people is wasted; I just don't know which half.' Relationships matter. How you engage with clients is critical to the evolution of your business. Having core values like karma that are lived and breathed will yield results. Mark and his team are testament to this.

A good culture can help you survive a bad strategy

Culture may all sound straightforward, but many organisations get it wrong. As psychologist Carol Dweck writes in her book *Mindset* (Dweck, 2017), energy company Enron was once the corporate poster child. Everything at Enron was about being the smartest person in the room. The hiring policy was entirely focused on talent; every hire was a go-getter.

A culture was created that worshipped talent, which forced employees to look and act as if they were extraordinarily talented.

People with such a mindset struggle to admit to their deficiencies or mistakes – they would rather lie about and hide them. The ultimate result was a multibillion-dollar bankruptcy and the biggest auditing failure in corporate history.

To Chris, it's important to continue to get smarter by fostering a culture of safety, creating an environment where people will tell the truth. His people won't get fired for making a mistake, but they will get fired for covering it up. He has been intentional about developing a culture where people are not afraid, because when people are afraid, they don't necessarily help themselves.

In healthy organisations, people learn from one another. They admit when they don't know, they identify critical issues, and as a result they recover quickly from mistakes.

Don't get stuck in an echo chamber

Human psychology tells us that we love being surrounded by people who look, sound and think similarly to ourselves. Think of the well-known proverb, 'Birds of a feather flock together.' Hiring people who 'get' your culture is vital, but success rests on you not taking a cookie cutter approach as it will only create homogenous teams. You want to hire to fit the culture, but that doesn't mean the same thinkers/exact fits. You don't want to look around the room and see your mirror image, nor do you want an echo chamber where you only hear your words coming back. Echo chambers are comfortable, but self-limiting.

As Michael puts it, 'There's no point in surrounding yourself with people who always agree with you, otherwise you may as well draw their salary and agree with yourself.' Chris concurs, saying, 'A collegial model is only valuable if you have diversity around the table.'

Stratospheric leaders and those who have achieved extraordinary success do not surround themselves with intellectual clones. They actively seek out diversity of thought and opinion and open themselves up to new ideas. They recognise that constructive contrarians offer thoughtful alternative views not to be polarising, but to accelerate progress. That is how they challenge their status quo and maximise the depth and range of their knowledge.

These leaders enrol their board members to provide challenge. The board members are not chosen, nor are they in their seats, to be passive. Healthy challenge is fundamental in taking the organisation to the next level.

One of the MarketAxess leadership team praises Rick for 'not just setting a board that is only gonna follow what Rick says'. Leaders often say they want to be challenged and I believe the ask is genuine, but my sense is that rarely do they *really* want it. Stratospheric leaders are the exceptions.

Where are you surrounding yourself with intellectual clones? How open are you to new ideas? Are you actively seeking out diversity of thought in your discussions?

Many of the obstacles in business today are not new. The ancient Romans might not have faced issues related to cybersecurity or corporate finance, but they did need to represent the voices and opinions of diverse groups, to be inclusive of different ideas from different people across the empire. Stratospheric CEOs will reference these historical intersections as being valuable learnings – whether it is Henry talking about the Roman Senate or Michael on military strategy. They study and learn from those who came before them on how and what they did.

Summary

If you want to understand culture in a single word, look no further than your *people*. Culture is a collective organisational character that is vital to success, and it all starts at the top.

A culture is a living organism that needs to be invested in, lived and breathed. The best and most successful companies have cultures that are deliberate and constantly evolving. Where the culture is right and everybody embodies the company's values, results will follow.

You want to establish your culture right from the start of your business, as it's difficult to change a culture once it's embedded. To do this, make sure you hire people not just for their skillsets, but also for their fit with your values. Do not look for an exact fit with you personally, though. If you don't have diversity throughout your teams, the constructive contrarians who will challenge the status quo and drive innovation, you will be existing in an echo chamber. This may be comfortable, but it will be fatal for your growth.

SEVEN

Self-Leadership

'You have to be able to hold up a mirror, to see what you can do better and how the world perceives you.'

Lee Olesky

Truly knowing yourself is a superpower. Some experts say it is the meta skill of the twenty-first century. Aristotle's words 'Knowing yourself is the beginning of all wisdom' are echoed by entrepreneur Steven Bartlett, who tweeted, 'There is no self-development without self-awareness. You can read as many books as you like, but if you're unable to read yourself you'll never learn a thing' (Bartlett, 2020). They both couldn't be more on point.

All effective leadership starts with self-leadership. According to psychologist Dr Tasha Eurich, 'Self-awareness is one of the most important determinants of success and failure' (Eurich, 2018), yet it remains a remarkably rare quality.

The question 'Who am I?' is seemingly simple, but it can be much harder to answer. Yet when we start to change the questions we ask ourselves (becoming more introspective), we change our experience of life. The invisible becomes visible.

Henry Fernandez states:

> 'You cannot be a great leader without self-awareness. Starting a company and leading a business is not easy and the biggest challenge isn't founding the company or taking on a new team. The question is can you stay in the company? Can you grow it? Can you develop it? Can you turn into a leader of the company and have people follow you?'

To truly answer these questions, we need to start with a willingness and a desire to hold the mirror up. This requires us to go within and *really* see ourselves, to understand ourselves from the inside out (who we are) and the outside in (other people's experience of us).

People can be self-centred or ego driven, limiting the aperture through which they see themselves, but becoming self-aware is a skill that can be learned. For those who are introspective by nature, it's a skill that can be refined and improved.

How do we become better at knowing ourselves?

Make time for self-reflection

The most important relationship we have is with ourselves, and yet it is often the most neglected. Self-reflection is a way of bolstering and harnessing that connection and processing the stuff that simply isn't serving us. Holding on to it carries weight, which others can't necessarily see, but we can feel.

I think of self-reflection much like spring cleaning a room in your home – maybe it's the sitting room. Picture opening its door. You walk through, pause and examine what's in there. As you look around, you notice what needs cleaning, organising, moving, storing or bidding farewell to. A room in your home, much like your mind, can be filled with clutter that is taking up valuable space. Reflection enables you to see things differently, to notice what you may be missing. It brings awareness, perspective and clarity.

While our stratospheric leaders don't liken their reflective time to cleaning their homes, they do refer to it as strategic thinking time and a valuable component in their leadership arsenal. Some people may regard self-reflection as having connotations of ego and pride, when in reality the ability to take the time to reflect is a key trait of successful leadership. It's an enabler for the lightbulb moments and a time to connect the creative dots. It's a place to step back, take stock and recalibrate.

Stratospheric leaders are purposeful about stepping out of the noise of life to gather perspective, to strategise and be intentional. It offers them the space to determine what they need to focus on and what needs their attention. Chris builds time to think into his schedule, referencing it as decompression and an opportunity to regroup. Lance Uggla likens it to playing cards. Self-reflection gives him the necessary space to think about the next move. Why play the ace of hearts now when the three of clubs will suffice?

As a leader, with the many demands on your time and attention, you could easily consider self-reflection to be expendable or have feelings of guilt around dedicated self time. After all, the concept of 'doing' is often driven by tasks; thinking and reflecting are not typically recognised. People are not paid for that. It's the materialised outcomes from the thinking that are ultimately valued.

However, our group of stratospheric CEOs don't see self-reflection as time out or an indulgence, but time invested. To achieve and deliver effectively, they recognise this reflective time needs to be respected. It's their boardroom away from the boardroom and an indispensable investment, and ultimately the business wins when the audacious goals that result are realised. As Chris shares, without self-reflection time, there would be fewer new ideas, poorer strategy, less self-care and less effective prioritisation.

Building the necessary stamina for the role

In Chapter One, I referred to leadership as akin to being an athlete. Corporate athletes can find themselves running daily marathons, especially when they don't have boundaries in place. Managing your energy, as well as your time, is one of the keys to the long game. It is likely we all recognise the real danger of burnout and chronic overwhelm, yet we can be complicit in actively creating the conditions we say we don't want through our actions. As Jeff Bezos says, 'We are our choices' (Bezos, 2018).

Self-knowledge, which comes from self-reflection, offers us valuable insight to understand which habits and activities are punitive versus restorative to our wellbeing and health. This means recognising our outlets for decompression and investing in them.

All the leaders featured in this book credit the value of sport on multiple levels. Not only in relation to equipping them with lessons learned around teamwork, creating wins as a unit, strategising, preparing for action, not panicking from a loss, learning from defeat, staying focused and taking on board feedback from multiple directions, but also the importance of physical fitness. 'Healthy body, healthy mind' is a mantra that they all share.

Rick McVey cites sport as an important mental outlet for creating long-term performance: 'The connection has always been so clear to me that in my times of stress, I work out more. That's what keeps me going.' Lee sees sport as a foundational pillar to ground himself and compartmentalise.

It can be easy to neglect exercise due to lack of prioritisation, or we may simply find ourselves with good intentions, but struggling to find time. In reality, endorphins and dopamine (nature's mood boosters) don't know if you have exercised for one hour or ten minutes. Your body needs the inputs of nutrition, rest and exercise to build stamina.

It's not a one-off task. Stamina is a long-term game, which needs consistency, thought and a commitment to it. Sport activities can be thought of as selfish, but they are *selfist*. Ultimately you are giving yourself what you need first, so you have more to give others and your business.

Building stamina can mitigate the risk of burnout. Lance says simply, 'People who burn out are taking on too much.' Although he hasn't fully experienced it, he has been on the edges, feeling the mental and physical fatigue where you think you can't go any further. He speaks of the importance of knowing yourself, so you take on just the right amount to avoid stepping into the place of diminishing returns.

This means knowing your body, listening to its whispers and recognising the associated feelings and behaviours when you are fatigued. You may feel it in your heart, in your breath, in your tiredness, in your diet. Are you fuelling yourself with junk food or jacking your system up on caffeine? Your body is always talking to you, if you choose to listen to it.

At the point of fatigue, stewardship sits with you to pull back. In Lance's words, 'It's reckless to allow yourself to burn out,' but it can seem to be hard to avoid it. You may be working on a deal or project and there just aren't enough hours in the day, and it needs you to drive it to the finish line. This requires you to know how to manage yourself. When you're getting close to burnout, you have to know it's there and take action.

Chris highlights the importance of having balance and being healthy to be productive at work. He suggests thinking about work as a lifecycle. There are periods in your working life that are intense, and others are a little calmer where you can have more flexibility. Leverage the latter when they come. Take advantage of time being enabled for other things and where possible, ensure that those periods are intentionally created.

Family time is fuel for the bigger picture

Several of the leaders profiled in this book speak about the cost of entrepreneurism. The relentless focus, discipline, pressure and intensity can lead to personal costs if left unchecked.

The time sacrificed (or some would say invested) in always being on, travelling and tired can ultimately impact the relationships with those closest to you. One leader said that in the early days of scaling his business, his family told him that the outside world saw the best of him, while they saw the rest of him. It's hard when you are living and breathing your vision for it not to become all-consuming as there are so many things pulling on your attention every day. Life in the entrepreneurial lane can seem exotic and dynamic – but it's a life your family may not be experiencing in the same way.

For several of our stratospheric leaders, whether it is in terms of health or relationships, there have been lessons learned along the way, often the hard way. If you are spending huge amounts of time away from your family, building and running a business, there will be an impact and cost. Being reflective and crystal clear on your priorities will draw the spotlight on to what needs your attention. What are you missing? What ultimately needs to change? The micro decisions, the quality of your presence, and your empathy and awareness towards those closest to you matter. Listen to their words, their signs and silent messaging. Don't miss the vital clues.

In this vein, Lance speaks of the importance of being intentional and the lessons he learned on the value of distributing your energy across all aspects of your life. This means actively building in downtime for relaxing, taking holidays, exercising, eating well and prioritising time with loved ones. In his words, 'All those things are really fuel for the bigger picture.'

Henry agrees about the importance of investing in these areas. For him, it serves to compound what drives his professional life and it keeps his mind clear too. He shares, 'Carving out time for family and friends is essential for maintaining those relationships. Time invested with them is a good reminder there is another part of life outside of work.'

Chris Willcox speaks of the importance of having activities or people that anchor you, be they hobbies, family or friends. It can be easy for work to be front and centre with everything else dropped in around that; it requires discipline to prioritise family and hobbies, and fit work around them.

It is important to note that all the leaders profiled in this book credit their upbringings and stable family lives as fuel for what they have gone on to create. Rick speaks of his family as having been a great support system for him and his siblings throughout their lives. There is such value when you feel loved and part of a unit. You have your trusted system around you to champion you, and to be your check and balance. Stratospheric leaders bring intentionality to make all the pieces of their lives fit.

Leadership is demanding

For our stratospheric leaders, it wasn't just about the number of hours of physical work they invested in the start-up phase, but also the mental hours to really get the business going. Burgeoning entrepreneurs shouldn't take this lightly. There can be such a buzz around entrepreneurship and building new businesses, the engine of all economies over time, but it can be underestimated how much work is involved and how few people are successful. This can create strain on your family and your other relationships because invariably, you are in the business 24/7.

Enrolling your family into a common understanding or clarity of expectations is so important – expectations around the hours you will be working, the time you will be travelling and the need for forgiveness when you will inevitably be distracted, preoccupied or not present emotionally and/or physically. Certainly, it won't all be plain sailing, so regular open communication with your family, friends and colleagues will be needed. Often, relationships – personal or professional – break down when people stop talking. A small niggle can soon fester and magnify into something far greater if left unattended.

Lance speaks of the importance of having a supportive partner. It can be scary and daunting starting up a business and leaving behind a job that has security and stability. After all, there is a real risk it won't work out. There are no guarantees, nor is there a crystal ball.

You may have faith, a belief and an inner confidence in your vision, but a belief isn't tangible and can be hard to quantify for others. You can effectively be throwing a grenade into a nice, safe and secure family life and turning it upside down. Sharing your belief around the idea and your ambition with your family may not mean they embody the same level of confidence as you, but acknowledging the inevitable sacrifices that they will be making, which could span multiple years, is an essential component in building the trust you will need them to have.

Win the morning, win the day

I've observed that, almost without exception, successful people start their day early. They create a powerful routine for first thing in the morning to set their priorities and intentions for the day. As a result, they tend to accomplish more in less time.

As Lee Olesky shares, 'When you harness the power of optimising your morning, you will genuinely find yourself operating on a higher plane for the rest of the day.'

Lance emphasises the benefit an early morning routine brings. 'If you find time to put in thirty minutes of exercise or meditation or reading or something in the morning before work, you will start with a better balance.'

It may seem easy in principle to get up early, and yet it is far harder in practice, but it's a skill worth honing. If you are rushing out of the shower, rushing to get your coffee and starting your day frenetically, you are already on the back foot. You simply won't be as effective.

Lance says he wants to be excited about the start of the day, so he advises you need to be ready early. If you're starting at 9am, you need to be in the office at 8:30, having your coffee, reading, collecting info, getting organised. If you have done some physical exercise, the endorphins will be working their magic and you will be starting your day with a more positive mindset.

For Henry, his morning comprises a little bit of visioning and thinking (he describes it as daydreaming), which he has done throughout his life. He asks himself, 'What decisions am I going to make today to move things forward? No more analysis, no more discussions, but the actual decisions.'

When I observe leaders, I am always looking for the difference that makes a difference. Where are the marginal gains? What are they prepared to do that others may be less willing to? What are their daily habits that lead to the big wins? How they start the day strongly determines the impact and influence they have and it's a habit we can all access and implement if we choose. These seemingly small things, executed consistently and with discipline, compound and add up over time.

Remove the WOMBATs

We all have good habits and bad habits. I think of bad habits as WOMBATs – wastes of money, brains and time. A bad habit may be mindlessly scrolling on social media, drinking that extra glass of wine in the evening or being unnecessarily hard on ourselves.

Your habits will drive you forward or hold you back/keep you stuck. Rick describes running and growing a public company as akin to being a professional athlete:

> 'You have to stay in shape and take care of yourself. You can't take your eye off the ball and start forming bad habits. Otherwise, you won't have the endurance and mental clarity that you need to manage a company and all the complexity that comes with it.'

This is where heightened self-awareness helps: being conscious of who or what your 'time sucks' are. Who are the energy vampires? What are better choices that may serve you? Ask yourself these questions, and then take action to rectify things.

Cultivating good habits requires you to do the work. As you engage in new habits and let the ones not serving you go, it's important to remind yourself that it will take practice, patience and purpose. It can take time to instil new habits as we vacillate between them and the old ones. Self-reflection will provide valuable insight on what's working and what's not. How are you holding yourself accountable to make your desired changes?

Be wary of the perception gap

You may not know about basketball, but you will likely have heard of Michael Jordan – star player of the Chicago Bulls. Jordan was a genius, a phenomenon. His point scoring was legendary and his ability to influence a game unparalleled. He was passionate about driving performance – both the team's and his own. He believed in leading by example.

When several of his teammates were asked to describe him for the Netflix series *The Last Dance* (Tollin, 2020), their answers were consistent. They admired and were in awe of him, but some referred to him as a bully, a tyrant. Even in the world of elite sport, he was considered aggressive.

When this feedback was shared with Jordan, he was shocked. 'I wanted to win, but I wanted them to win and be a part of that as well,' he explained.

One cannot doubt Jordan's impact, but he had a big blind spot. He believed he was a passionate leader, his teammates felt differently. Jordan knew his intent, which was a good one, but in the absence of that being transparent, he could only be judged by his actions and behaviours (ie that which was visible to his teammates).

Jordan may have been unique, but his leadership challenges were not. We can have the best of intentions about how we want to be perceived, yet a big gap can exist (sometimes as wide as the Grand Canyon) between our desired perception and the reality experienced by others. This stresses the importance of soliciting feedback regularly to capture data and insight on what the real experience of your people is. What is it really like to work for you? How do you make people feel when you walk into the room? How accessible are you? How safe do people feel sharing the uncomfortable truths?

The challenge for many leaders is that they struggle to obtain honest and constructive feedback, not necessarily due to a lack of asking, but because people want to give them the polished apple due to their title. Humans often don't like being the truth tellers. We want to be liked, so there can be huge discomfort in sharing what we believe (or perceive) if it's a message the other person may not want or be open to hearing.

Satya Nadella (executive chairman and CEO of Microsoft) talks of the know-it-all leader versus the learn-it-all leader (Nadella, 2019). The learn-it-all leader recognises the limitless journey of learning. All the leaders profiled in this book subscribe to the Japanese philosophy of *kaizen* – continuous learning and a mentality of always being curious. They are active in asking the incisive questions and then showing that they are taking action. There is always something to learn, something to improve on.

Dr Carol Dweck's well-known work *Mindset* (Dweck, 2017) explains how a fixed mindset will lead to stagnation, while a growth mindset can unlock potential futures that are currently beyond our imagination. You can manage your mindset – that is within your gift. Be ready to learn, be curious about what you don't know and seek out lessons every day.

Linked to the perception gap are blind spots. Blind spots could be hidden talents or areas for development that are by definition known to others, but unknown to you. It did make me smile when one leader I worked with (not one of our stratospheric CEOs) declared he knew all his blind spots.

I once worked with a leader who would spend meetings pacing the room, while all his colleagues were seated. It was distracting and made others feel like they were back at school. He had no idea. I have observed leaders on their phones while in team meetings, leaving others around the table feeling their opinion or contribution was not listened to or valued.

A learn-it-all leader seeks to uncover their blind spots. Observing the room, reading the reactions of others, soliciting feedback will give you meaningful data points to determine which behaviours to dial up or down to achieve the impact you desire.

Realistic optimism

There is a ripple of impact created by everything you do – every action, every word, every gesture – that has a multiplier effect. How you show up sets the tone. An optimistic mindset breeds engagement.

In the early days of your business, it is all about you. Investors, clients and colleagues bet on the jockey, not the horse. They decide whether they invest their resources, capital or time with *you*. They want to see a leader who shows they can win, that they have the drive, resilience, fortitude and energy to do what it takes. They also want to see you are a leader who is open to learning, who can grow from feedback, who has the humility to admit what you don't know. The more of this you bring, the more your leadership role, your success, your impact and influence typically expand. This means that ultimately, self-leadership creates a virtuous circle. It can literally lead you to run a bigger, better business.

Shotscope.com data shows that 84% of amateur golfers will miss a putt short of the target (Shot Scope, 2023). According to W Timothy Gallwey in *The Inner Game of Golf* (Gallwey, 2015), this is not because they are incapable of hitting it further; it's because of self-doubt. They worry about everything that could go wrong, and so their body becomes less efficient and less fluid, which maximises the chances of hitting a poor (in this case short) shot.

When you think about entrepreneurs, founders of companies and leaders, to make progress and to create value, they are invariably on the borderline, questioning. Is this a good decision? Is this a good acquisition? Is this a good product? Is it a bad one? Is this the right time?

As Henry shares, 'You're always experiencing some level of self-doubt, so the most important thing is how you balance out the doubts versus the conviction.' It's not about whether you have self-doubt or not; it's about how you deal with the tug of war between the conviction and the doubts. How do you resolve that? How do you become comfortable with self-doubt? It's seldom that you're 100% convinced about something.

Rick agrees that moments of self-doubt come with the key decisions. In my work coaching C-suite leaders, I am yet to partner with someone who doesn't experience self-doubt. In my early career, I wrongly assumed the voice of the inner critic would diminish the higher you rose, yet in the overachieving realms, the voice typically gets louder as you progress into new, less comfortable and more unfamiliar zones.

What defines stratospheric leaders is not getting lost in the unhelpful thinking or ruminating on the things outside their control. They capture the unhelpful thinking and take action rather than getting stuck there. A huge dose of curiosity helps. When you make mistakes, you learn, move on and don't dwell on them.

As Michael shares:

> 'If you are always convinced of your own infallibility, you will one day come an almighty cropper. Nobody is

infallible. Confidence is, of course, essential, valuable and important, but overconfidence and certainty in your course of action is never advised.'

Maybe a good dose of doubt is in fact healthy!

Create a trusted tribe

Leadership can feel incredibly lonely, because ultimately you decide. Yes, you have teams and people around you, yet it can still seem isolating at the top. All the pressure, particularly when there are tough times, is on your shoulders, regardless of how good the team around you is, but there is a discernible difference between *feeling* alone and actually *being* alone.

It could be assumed that leaders, given their lifestyles and incomes, have fewer life concerns than most of us. This would be an unfair assumption. In addition to leading companies, leaders may have aging parents, have worries about their children's futures, be dealing with family sickness or managing the impact of stress on their own health and nervous systems, just like anyone else. Behind every title is a human and as such, leaders have days where they move mountains and days where they wobble. They are not infallible.

Surrounding yourself with a trusted tribe will give you a place to have the conversations you don't get to have elsewhere, enabling you to stay grounded. The tribe should include people you trust who have your best interests at heart – friends, family members and colleagues. This gives you a much-needed place where you can unload, release the pressure valve and vent. A place where you can have the unfiltered discussions and show up as yourself, not as your title, without consequences.

As Chris says, 'These are people who will give you the direct feedback and will tell you when you are wrong.' We all need truth tellers in our tribe. When you trust those giving you the feedback, you know the message is shared honestly and with positive intent, for your benefit.

We are meant to enjoy and experience life, not simply endure it. Life can sometimes test and push us to our outer edges, yet we have each got through 100% of our toughest days. Having your trusted tribe of confidants who will hold the mirror up and help you zoom out is critical.

Your tribe can be a lifeline. Nobody is an island. We are not meant to experience life alone.

Summary

Stratospheric leaders come from a place of self-mastery – a twinning of heightened self-awareness with acknowledgement of their impact on others. With self-knowledge comes the potential for exceptional leadership. It has a huge bearing on how we draw out the best in ourselves and others.

Fostering internal and external self-awareness takes time and it isn't a one-and-done learning experience. The internal questioning of who you are, what matters to you and what triggers you can be a life's work. It's a continual process of looking inward that requires time for self-reflection and for soliciting honest feedback.

Holding the mirror up and really seeing yourself is easy to speak of abstractly, but rarely done well or even done at all. Ultimately, you are the CEO of your own life and the decisions you make impact your broader stakeholders and community. Interlocking ambition and the desire to succeed with the honest acknowledgement of what you need to do will ultimately create the version of yourself that your self-reflection is driving towards. It's how ambitious visions are realised and the WIGs achieved.

PART TWO

APPLYING THE LEARNING

In Part Two, I would like to recap on the learnings shared by our stratospheric CEOs in each chapter of Part One. I will then highlight the particular lessons I took from each chapter, including some of the ways I and my clients have applied this valuable learning.

Lessons: One

An Audacious Vision

In Chapter One, 'An Audacious Vision', we looked at:

- **Enabling daydreaming** – training our brains to create and innovate.

- **Connecting, collecting and learning** – what will your business look like in one year, five years, ten years? Constant learning is essential to enable its growth.

- **Intentional innovation** – visualise the future so you can innovate for change proactively rather than reactively.

- **Ambitious goals** – leaders who set audacious goals have the advantage over those who remain more realistic.

- **Communicate your audacity** with all your stakeholders – your teams and your clients.

- **Be discerning in who you listen to** – surround yourself with those who challenge you positively and lift you up. Get those energy vampires out of your life, they're doing you no good at all.

Make time to daydream

A theme all the stratospheric CEOs shared when it comes to creating an audacious vision is that they are highly deliberate about carving out time for strategic thinking. They regard this not as time out, but as time invested. Henry Fernandez says, 'I make time to daydream,' and I absolutely love his choice of words. Daydreaming for him is a hobby and passion where he thinks about trends, change and transformation.

Taking time to daydream is not childish, but childlike. Children look at the world with curiosity and open eyes, which is the essence of creativity, but our curiosity can sometimes get eroded the older we get.

Daydreaming applies as much to our personal lives as it does to our professional ones. Where could you be more childlike today?

What can we learn from stratospheric leaders?

- **Make time to daydream** to see the future and evolution of things, and then work the present to achieve the future.

- **Be curious and make time to marvel.** This is where new ideas, creativity and concepts come from.

- **Know where and how you do your best blue-sky thinking** – is it a certain place, time of day, during a specific activity?

- **A different way of doing things can lead to the same high-quality output.** Leaders don't have a monopoly on all the best ideas, so listen to the input of all your people.

Applying the learning

- Take time to contemplate your dreams.

- Go exploring, see where every path takes you and don't be afraid to go back if you need to.

- Ask, 'How big could/should this be?' A great question from a go-to-market perspective.

- Ask, 'What are we not doing?' A great question from an ongoing marketing perspective.

Audacious goals and luck

Stratospheric leaders are highly intentional individuals who set BHAGs and WIGs. They believe that the size and scope of their dreams give them an advantage over those who set more easily realisable goals. Mediocre goals create mediocre outcomes.

What can we learn from stratospheric leaders?

- **Look beyond.** While practical, realistic goals are part of their business success, it is their vision, ability to see beyond the obvious and desire to reach for the stars that set stratospheric CEOs apart from others. As Lance Uggla confirms, 'My whole management style is to set audacious goals and work really hard to reach them. You need to have goals that are inspirational and you need to believe in them. You have to dream where you are going.'

- **Embrace lucky breaks.** Stratospheric leaders acknowledge the element and influence of luck. They know there have been lots of great ideas that have fallen by the wayside and good people running new companies who didn't make it. As Rick McVey explains, 'Sometimes you get breaks at key times that help you keep going and move forward, and other times you don't. It's nice to have some luck, because it gives everybody hope that they can be a bit lucky too.'

- **Success is not linear.** The journey from A to B is seldom straightforward and often winds its way through rocky terrain and boggy ground. Finding ways to manoeuvre through and beyond these challenges is a skill to nurture and grow.

Applying the learning

- Appreciate that mistakes and failures can teach you more than you might recognise at first.

- Embrace the unknown.

- Use your dream and vision as your map to remind yourself where you are heading whenever you feel a little lost.

Stay focused

In my work with stratospheric leaders, one challenge is deciphering the great ideas from the good. You don't need hundreds of wins. One or two significant successes can have a huge impact, so you need to work out the things that truly matter.

What can we learn from stratospheric leaders?

- **Ruthlessly prioritise** – you don't need extra time, you need more focus.

- **Eliminate distractions** – no more mindless scrolling through your socials.

- **Understand the distinction** between what *could* be done and what *should* be done.

- **Look for the one high watermark, not the average**. Your top investment can be worth more than the total of all your other investments. Investment can mean your time, energy, effort, budget, focus, resources.

- **Don't get sidetracked by shiny objects**. That so-called silver bullet will dilute your attention, and that of your management team and employees.

- **Be disciplined** – discipline and focus create opportunity.

Applying the learning

- Keep your lines of communication with your stakeholders open. How clear are you on your priorities? How clear are those around you?

- Where is your attention being diluted? Which distractions could you eliminate? Who are the champions and who are the energy vampires?

- Ask, 'What should be done?' When you're looking at your current tasks/activities, which are *really* adding value?

Lessons: Two

Risk Is Possibility

In Chapter Two, the lessons our stratospheric CEOs shared included:

- **Every risk has to be calculated** – stratospheric leaders don't make decisions on impulse; they seek to understand the risk and evaluate the value they can create.

- **Decisions are rarely black and white** – sometimes you will need to make a decision without having all the relevant information. Don't delay too long, especially in a time of crisis. It's far better to make a decision and then refine it than not to make a decision and fall behind the innovators in your industry.

- **The importance of mindsets and perceptions** – will you stay comfortable, or will you develop the mindset to go out and seek new opportunities, perhaps even make your own?

- **The importance of communicating confidence internally and externally** – there is a reason why people talk about consumer confidence. Stratospheric leaders instil confidence across their stakeholders and have confidence in their dreams.

- **Don't be scared of being scared** – healthy pressure will provide the necessary challenge and focus. If we take archery as an analogy, it is the drawing tight of the bow string that provides the tension for the arrow to hit the bullseye.

- **Reframing failure as learning** – how will you and your people innovate if you don't learn the lessons from your mistakes? Be sure to create an environment where it's OK to fail; the essential part is to learn from it and improve.

- **Intuition versus analysis** – stratospheric leaders usually know instinctively when something feels right, but by taking a moment to reflect and ask questions, and by listening to their confidants, they reduce the risk of failure.

- **Momentum is key** – once you're on the right path, keep going. Keep learning, keep failing, keep improving, keep innovating.

Learn the lessons

Extraordinary leaders have a close relationship with failure. Kobe Bryant missed more shots than any other basketball player – 14,481 in total (Levy, 2022) – yet he is number four on the all-time scoring leader board. Failure isn't an alternative to success, but a prerequisite to achieving it. Similarly, the margin between something working and not working is not always that great.

Failure can be painful. You will have moments of insecurity, pockets of paranoia and times of self-doubt. When this happens, reflect on the lessons you've learned.

What can we learn from stratospheric leaders?

- **Experience is the hardest teacher.** It gives you the test first and the lesson afterwards. Be sure to spend more time on the lesson and less time ruminating about the test.

- **Failure gives feedback.** Have the willingness and tenacity to investigate the lessons. Exploit the opportunity to evaluate what you would have done differently.

- **As a leader, own your mistakes.** It will encourage others to do the same.

- **Create a safe environment.** In an environment that encourages people to take calculated risks, allow them to talk about their shortcomings, as mistakes *will* happen. You can only eliminate mistakes if you discuss them.

Applying the learning

- When you experience a setback, how much time do you invest reflecting on what happened and what led to those mistakes? How can you ensure you are better prepared next time?

- With the lens of hindsight, what is one failure that has given you your biggest learnings?

Great leaders ask great questions

One of the observable skills that differentiates stratospheric leaders is that they are voracious learners. They seek to learn from every situation, and they are masterful in the art of asking good questions at the right time.

Rather than expressing assumptions and suggestions or vague wishes disguised as questions, they ask short, open, incisive, clear questions to get high-quality inputs for their decision making. Being intellectually curious and open minded is how they turn thoughts into potentially game-changing ideas. It is also how they get their teams to think.

What can we learn from stratospheric leaders?

What does a good question look like? These powerful questions from stratospheric leaders can be applied to your business or team, and some are equally relevant for self-reflection:

- If there is one thing we are missing here, what would it be?

- If the business had a voice, what would it be saying?

- What counts that we are not counting?

- What do we do differently from our competitors? Does this help or hinder us?

- If we knew we couldn't fail, what would we try?

- How are we spending our time? Where is the greatest impact of our time today?

- If we are saying yes to this, what are we saying no to?

- What prevents us from making the changes we know will make us even more effective?

Applying the learning

- Are you as a leader changing as quickly as the world around you? High-quality questions will help you.

- Ask 'tell me… explain… describe…' questions. Questions without a question mark are non-threatening and designed to solicit more information.

- Given questions do the heavy lifting in communication, how much thought are you giving to the ones you ask?

Pay attention to your intuition

The power of intuition is not often discussed, but it has an important role alongside data-based analysis and logic. Wisdom is not something we can strive to acquire, but if we slow down, we can notice what is already there.

What can we learn from stratospheric leaders?

- **Decide quickly, then refine.** An organisation is often much better served by a fast decision.

- **Timely action.** Failure to act can lead to stagnation and missed opportunities, poor morale and frustration among the team.

- **Learn from everything.** Sometimes things won't work out *and* you will be wiser from the experience.

- **Lean back on experience.** Intuition is a distillation of all your experiences. The gut seldom comes out of nowhere. It is probable that you have dealt with something similar before. Take a moment to step back and consider this at the same time as paying attention to what your gut tells you. What happened before? What did you do and what could you apply to this situation?

- **Don't let perfect be the enemy of good.** Don't be afraid to make a mistake. Following your instinct means not being too defensive in your strategy. Real innovation comes from the science of 'this might not work'.

Applying the learning

- How often are you taking time to listen to your intuition? When the next decision-making moment arises, what more could you do to pay attention to your intuition as well as your cognition?

- Where have you trusted your gut and it has led to an amazing outcome?

- Reflecting back, when have you missed out by ignoring your intuition? How will you apply what you learned from this?

Intuition versus analysis

Henry Fernandez highlights the importance of using intuition versus analysis in decision making. There are times when the situation requires all the variables, but collecting all the inputs and allowing your left brain (the analytical side) to drive can lead to stagnation and missed opportunities.

What can we learn from stratospheric leaders?

- **Trust your gut.** If you feel something is right, then listen to what it is saying – even if you later overrule it with your head.

- **There is power in the pause.** Take a moment to reflect, tapping into your intuition, ingenuity and experience.

- **Find a quiet space.** When you need a quick decision and you don't have all the information to hand, find a quiet space and listen to your internal voice.

Applying the learning

Ask yourself:

- 'Is this a decision I need to bring data, theory and my analytical brain to, or is this a decision for my instinct and intuition?'

- 'Is this a reversible or an irreversible decision? Can it be undone or is it one to live and die by?'

- 'Have I dealt with something similar before? What did I do? What was the result? What could I apply to this situation?'

Lessons: Three

Execution

Let's recall what our stratospheric leaders taught us in Chapter Three:

- **Be an execution jockey.** When you show you can execute your vision, it gives your collective stakeholders confidence. It also serves to attract more A players.

- **Clearly define and communicate your execution objectives.** Successful execution of a vision requires clearly defined objectives and a structured series of steps and pathways. Clarity will minimise any ambiguity.

- **Discern between could and should.** Differentiate between what *could* be done and what *should* be done.

- **Be agile.** Success generally will be achieved not by doggedly following your first set of goals, but by your agility.

- **Surf often, snorkel sometimes, scuba by appointment.** This delightful metaphor was donated by Brad Levy, CEO of Symphony. As a leader, you should surf by nature, snorkel regularly to look below the surface while recognising when to scuba for the deeper dive. Operating at a high level (surfing) will require you to build processes to enable this.

- **Be deliberate in measuring progress.** Stratospheric leaders have a clear execution plan and are deliberate about measuring progress regularly against their goals and budget. As the unknowns become known, they then make the necessary changes as they go.

- **Exercise patient urgency.** There are times where slowing down with intention and purpose will help you make sound, high-impact decisions and maintain emotional balance. Crucially, it will also reduce your and your team's chances of burning out.

- **'Lucky' execution.** All the stratospheric leaders in this book attribute a portion of their success to luck. Lance Uggla shares that it's good to allow yourself to pause every once in a while and go, 'Geez, I'm really lucky to be here.'

- **Celebrate the wins.** It's important to acknowledge and celebrate the mini wins and the significant moments along the execution journey.

- **Customer-centric focus.** A customer's experience of you and your business is key. If you are customer centric, this means seeing them as partners and actively investing in and valuing your relationships with them.

Generating new ideas is easy; executing them is hard

An idea needs to be transformed into reality for it to have value. This applies as much in the boardroom as it does in everyday life.

My observation of stratospheric leaders is that they and their teams are what I like to call execution jockeys.

What can we learn from stratospheric leaders?

- **Great thoughts are just that.** They only matter if you execute against them.

- **Hire execution jockeys.** When hiring a leader (at any level), look for evidence that they have executed in other businesses.

- **Ruthlessly prioritise.** Set your team clear objectives and keep them simple. If you give people a dozen things to do, the odds of them executing them all go down.

- **Execution is ongoing and iterative.** Create a constant feedback loop to give you crisper execution.

- **Measure as you go.** Be deliberate on measuring progress and do it often.

- **Be unwavering.** Execution is hard and you need mental toughness to stick with it.

- **Clearly articulate your message.** If you can't sell your idea, you're not going to win. Be clear and consistent both internally and externally.

- **Everything is hard before it is easy.** The day before anything is a breakthrough, it's a stupid idea.

Applying the learning

- How much time are you spending on ideation versus execution?

- How clear are you on the long-term vision for your business? How clear are others?

- Do you have a constant feedback loop?

- How clear is your team on what you want them to do?

Exercise patient urgency

Success takes time and patience. Things will go wrong. You and those around you will make mistakes, obstacles will appear and sometimes they will feel insurmountable. As Lance Uggla shared, 'You don't become a world champion Formula 1 driver if you haven't crashed a few cars.'

Determination is the quality to cultivate when you're faced with failure. Failures are simply setbacks and a setback only counts as a failure if you don't learn the lesson it has to offer.

What can we learn from stratospheric leaders?

- **Never give in.** Tough times don't last – tough people do.

- **Your worst professional experience can become your most important defining experience.** The Finnish word *sisu* speaks of the mental strength to continue to try even after you feel you've reached your limit.

- **Don't be discouraged** from aiming for something you feel passionate about. There will always be somebody on the sidelines scrutinising or doubting your vision.

- **Make new mistakes.** Don't repeat old ones.

- **Learn from your mistakes.** Be constructive in your critical evaluation and take on board what the setback has to teach you. Rumination on the setback itself is unhelpful and can keep you stuck.

- **Challenges test and strengthen you.** Scar tissue is stronger than normal tissue. Failure makes us stronger if we learn from it rather than being shamed into inaction by it.

Applying the learning

- Take time to make sense of the event. What have you learned to ensure this won't happen again?

- What will you do differently next time for a better outcome?

- Apparent failures can set you up for later success. Looking back at your career dips, what can you learn that could help you going forward?

- If being open to failure was fundamental to your success, what would you do differently?

Observe, orientate, decide, act

Remember the US Navy SEALs' adage, 'Slow is smooth and smooth is fast'? This allows them to assess a situation and put a preliminary plan into action. When things are smooth, they can then move faster.

This links to Newton's third law of motion: 'To every action there is an equal and opposite reaction'. The faster you try to go, the more pushback you get and the greater the resistance you face. While it may seem counterintuitive to slow down when you're heading for the stratosphere, that may be what the situation most needs.

What can we learn from stratospheric leaders?

- **Slowing down with purpose will help you make sound, high-impact decisions.** It will help you maintain emotional balance, allow you to sustain and keep you from burning out.

- **Creating space gives you the opportunity to scan, study and observe.** You will notice more and recognise patterns and themes. It also allows for a course-correction, if needed.

- **Take a moment before you react.** This enables you to make a considered response rather than a knee-jerk reaction.

- **Be focused with your time.** Ask yourself, 'Is this the most important thing I could be doing with my time and resources right now?' Slow down and spend time working out what matters. What is the best use of your time?

- ***Gradarius Firmus Victoria.*** This is not from a stratospheric leader, but the Latin motto of the AFC Richmond Team in the TV series *Ted Lasso* (Sudeikis et al, 2020). It is translated as 'taking little steps towards victory', ie having audacious goals and always making progress to achieve them.

Applying the learning

- How much time do you spend observing and planning before deciding and acting?

- What speed do you typically operate at?

- What could be the positive consequences of a change in pace?

Lessons: Four

Global Crisis Management

The world has never been more complex, chaotic and unpredictable. News no longer happens to other people. It is no longer a distant occurrence. Humankind has entered a new paradigm where heightened disruption has become our prevailing reality.

Before we focus on specific lessons around managing global crises from our stratospheric leaders and how we can put them into action, let's briefly recap on Chapter Four:

- **Don't panic.** In crisis events, stratospheric leaders are not looking around to see what everyone else is doing. Instead, they are making quick decisions that are focused on their market, their business and their people.

- **Control what you can control.** There are many things outside of your control, given the unpredictable nature of events. You can, however, control your response, attitude and mindset. This means giving thought to the energy you are radiating out.

- **Assemble a small crisis-management team.** In times of crisis, stratospheric leaders bring together a small, select group with different vantage points and perspectives to help determine the best approach, strategy and response, given the information available.

- **Decision making in the grey zone.** The first thing that you have to figure out is, which decisions are irreversible and which can be quickly changed if they turn out to be wrong?

- **Be visible.** Your people will value honesty and thoughtfulness.

- **Exercise behavioural range.** There is the what and the how of leadership – what you do in moments of crisis and how you do it. What is the energy you are using to convey your message? I call this behavioural range.

- **Tough times can be the differentiators.** Henry Fernandez likens business to a boat. If conditions are calm, it's hard to differentiate. It's in the stormy seas where you can stand out.

- **Good business requires empathy.** Modern-day leadership requires us to be more human, and empathy is not only a superpower, it's also a key requirement. It brings out the best in people, which ultimately is good for business.

Navigating the inevitable challenges

Managing unpredictability and uncertainty isn't new for leaders. Change has always been a constant companion, but what sets today's challenge apart is the speed of change, its relentlessness and the variability of outcomes to contend with.

How do we as leaders equip ourselves to navigate the inevitable challenges rather than simply bouncing from one crisis to the next?

What can we learn from stratospheric leaders?

- **Solutions don't come from pushing.** Pausing buys you time. Decisions become more thoughtful, less mistakes are made, better solutions are created.

- **Nothing in nature rushes, yet everything gets done.** Slow down. Sometimes slowly is the fastest way and zooming out will offer greater perspective.

- **Control what you can control.** As the title of author Charles Swindoll's book tells us, *Life Is 10% What Happens to You and 90% How You React* (Swindoll, 2023). There is a big difference between a knee-jerk reaction and a considered response with potentially two very different outcomes.

- **Time doesn't offer refunds.** Your time is a precious and non-renewable resource. Be mindful of its highest and best use. Don't let others steal time from you. Equally, don't freely give it away. For every yes, you are saying no to something else.

- **Maintain a trusted inner circle.** Leadership can be lonely, but there is a difference between feeling alone and being alone. It's OK not to be OK. You don't have to bury your emotions and pretend they don't exist. We all need a place to vent, an outlet for releasing the pressure valve and taking the corporate mask off free from judgement.

- **Being perfect as a leader isn't a realistic benchmark.** Strive for effectiveness instead. You are expected to acknowledge events unfolding in the world. It's important not to be silent, but as your written and spoken words will become evergreen and may be judged retrospectively, keep communication succinct.

Applying the learning

- Do you have a trusted inner circle with whom you can share frustrations or challenges? Who's in it? Who needs to be?

- Where are you wasting time ruminating on things that are outside of your control?

- If you are saying yes to this [invite, person, project etc], what are you saying no to?

It's not the plane, it's the pilot

There is a memorable scene in the film *Top Gun: Maverick* (Kosinski, 2022) when Tom Cruise's character first addresses his class of elite F18 fighter pilots. He holds up a thick wad of paper, the F18 manual, and asks them how well they know it. The pilots are gleeful as they confirm how they have consigned its contents to memory. He then promptly drops the manual in the bin to a loud clang and a collection of raised eyebrows.

This is an apt metaphor for the modern leader. The old 'manual' of leadership contained a relatively single-threaded list of contents: profit, growth, shareholder value. Command and control, authority and the promise of future bonuses and promotions would have probably been the sum of the remaining chapters.

However, today's leaders are operating in a far more complex and nuanced environment where the demands and expectations of employees, in particular, have evolved markedly. To attract and retain the best and brightest now requires human-centric leadership. You are expected not only to hit the numbers, but to do it while championing an environment of purpose, balance, flexibility, compassion and sustainability for your people. Oh, and if you make a mistake, be assured that you will be judged quickly and harshly.

The new leadership playbook starts with self or, to put it another way, the 'being' state of leadership. To thrive in a multi-threaded world requires you to master your mindset and your emotional state. As Maverick says in a later scene in the film, 'It's not the plane, it's the pilot'.

What can we learn from stratospheric leaders?

- **Make preparation around your emotional state and quality of presence a priority.** How will you arrive in the room? How do you want people to feel on hearing you? Knowing that, how do you need to be?

- **Understand the impact your behaviour and actions have on others.** Emotions are contagious.

- **Leaders set the tone.** Be intentional with the mood you want to create. How are you communicating? What does your body language say?

- **Know your hot buttons.** We will all be triggered at times. The sooner you understand your triggers, the sooner you can make a different choice as to how you are going to respond.

- **Anticipate the environment** so you can prepare and stay on track as the leader in the room.

- **Review.** See every opportunity as a learning event. What's working/not working? What could you do differently next time?

- **Have a confidant in your tribe** – somebody you can vent to. We all need to release the pressure valve at times.

- **Have a truth teller in your tribe.** Equally, you need a person who will give you the feedback others may not feel comfortable sharing. You can't improve on the things you don't know about.

Applying the learning

- Have others ever misread your feelings or thoughts?

- How aware are you of your mood and the impact it has on people?

- If you could invoke *one* word in people's minds, what would that be?

How to make decisions when everything is moving so fast

For a leader, making decisions with incomplete information and imperfect data is nothing new. What has changed is the pace and intensity of this decision making, set against a backdrop of increased scrutiny and judgement. Seemingly the stakes are bigger, the environment more complex and the number of competing priorities has increased.

How do you make timely decisions in today's world? How do you improve the odds of getting these decisions right?

What can we learn from stratospheric leaders?

- **Not all decisions are created equal.** Discern between those decisions that merit consideration, consultation and data, and those that really don't.

- **Guard against confirmation bias.** Recognise when you are seeking information simply to confirm your own view.

- **Recognise when undesirable emotions are present.** Being emotionally hijacked will influence the quality of your decision making.

- **Be wary of knee-jerk reactions.** There is a discernible difference between a considered response (even one based on gut and intuition) and a knee-jerk reaction.

- **Seek to learn what you may be missing.** What corners have you not looked around?

- **Be mindful of whose input you ask for.** Do the people around you bring a different vantage point or are they merely an echo chamber?

- **Zoom out.** Like a camera, widen the aperture on how you are looking at the situation to give greater perspective.

- **Choose the first good-enough option.** In time-pressured situations, this may be the best strategy. A wrong decision subsequently course-corrected is often better than no decision at all.

Applying the learning

- Whose voice(s) that need to be heard are you not listening to?

- Are you soliciting and truly hearing opposing points of view?

- What are you missing? What questions are you not asking?

Leading Others

This is a vast subject, especially in today's complex world, which is why Chapter Five is markedly longer than the others. It's one of the many things our stratospheric CEOs excel at, so let's remind ourselves what they taught us about leading other people:

- **Assemble a world-class leadership team.** Stratospheric leaders surround themselves with individuals who have different skills, views, opinions, styles and backgrounds. This enables broader perspectives and allows for more balanced decisions.

- **Get to know your team.** The more you know about people, the more you can trust them. By getting to know how they tick, you have their markers and can connect to the part of yourself that is going to resonate best with them.

- **Don't be afraid to make changes.** As it grows, the business will need different skills in different seats at different stages, which may mean moving people around and letting others go.

ppens when a good hire doesn't work out?
ou make the decision to let someone go, don't delay.
n how you plan to deliver the message, putting
you. lf in their shoes. Preparation is key to ensuring the
conversation goes as smoothly as possible.

- **Regularly evaluate your bench strength.** Understand what the business needs and hire the people who are potentially smarter than you or have the skills you don't. Their skills complementing yours will make you a better leader, so everyone can win.

- **Plan for succession.** Who could do each role in the business if they were given a chance? How willing would they be to take over as the successor with an unknown timeframe?

- **Stratospheric leaders delegate.** Delegation requires you to be honest with the things you don't know or are not the expert on. If you trust you have the right people, you can trust them to act.

- **Be clear in your expectations.** Everyone associates different meanings with different words. For example, does urgent mean today or this week? Keep your communications succinct and ensure everyone has understood everything.

- **Your people first, and then the customer.** It'll be your people who facilitate your business's relationships with your customers, hence the importance of intentionality around hiring a world-class team with cultural fit, and not just hiring for competence and capability.

- **Motivating those around you.** If you want positivity, passion and enthusiasm to radiate out, they're what you as a leader have to bring. It's a real leadership skill to stay positive, so it needs to be practised.

- **Listen to your teams.** Human beings can do a great job of having the corporate mask firmly welded on, appearing calm and controlled on the outside when they're overwhelmed or stressed on the inside.

- **Make mistakes, but learn from them.** You need to ensure people have the confidence to share their ideas and decisions, comfortable in the knowledge they may not work out.

- **Don't be the chatterbox.** *Silent* and *listen* have the same letters. It is so easy to underestimate the importance of listening. It is an active behaviour, not a passive response.

- **Understand people.** When it comes to relationships, we tend to get back what we put in. Leaders are in the business of people and a way to achieve high-quality connection with another person is through showing authentic interest in them.

- **Crucial conversations.** It's important to think of the conversations no one really enjoys as crucial rather than difficult or awkward, to put yourself in the right mindset. Preparation enables you to practise the inevitable discomfort, getting comfortable with the uncomfortable.

- **Receiving feedback.** Feedback, when it's executed in the right way, is a gift and a valuable learning opportunity. You don't know what you don't know, and we all have developmental areas and room for improvement.

- **Managing differences of opinion.** Everyone in a business sees things in a different way. It is the job of the leader to ensure that every point of view is represented, because none is complete without the others.

Now it's time to focus on the key learnings from this chapter and how best to apply them in your business.

Are you pushing your team too hard?

For most of us, working long hours is nothing new. What is different in the modern workplace is the pace, dynamism and intensity of those hours. We are all trying to sprint a marathon, and as a result pressure and stress are never far away.

Knowing this, as a leader, how do you drive your team to produce their best work, without pushing them beyond their capacity?

What can we learn from stratospheric leaders?

- **Awareness is foundational.** This means *really* knowing the people in your team and recognising the early signs of overwhelm such as irritability, impatience, being more emotionally triggered than usual and looking exhausted.

- **Safety is foundational.** This means creating an environment where your people feel able to put their hands up when things get too much rather than suffering in silence.

- **Be mindful of the behaviour you are modelling** and, inadvertently, the expectations you are setting. Your capacity doesn't equal your people's capacity. Based on the law of averages, they won't necessarily be as driven or focused as you (the leader).

- **Stress is inversely correlated to autonomy.** By empowering your people and delegating influence and decision making, you will give them more control. More control typically equates to less stress.

- **Create an agreement.** Ask your people to share openly with you if they find themselves stuck in survival mode. As a leader, you are not a mind reader and you can only act on the information available to you.

- **Be consistent in your messaging and your actions.** If you tell your people to take a break/holiday, don't then contact them during that time and expect a response.

- **Be ruthless in your own prioritisation** before enlisting help from members of your team. Not every task or issue is urgent and important.

- **Flex your empathy muscle.** Your people may have issues, passions and priorities outside of work that mean their capacity will be lower than yours. Be OK with that.

Applying the learning

- How will you know if you are pushing your people too far? What will you notice in their actions and behaviours?'

- Where can you delegate more decision making to your team?

- What behaviours around work–life balance and boundaries are you modelling to your team?

How to have the crucial conversations

Picture the scene. Someone just doesn't get you. They're picking holes in your arguments. In a meeting, they're clearly sceptical when you speak.

You've likely been in this situation more than once. Be honest – how does that make you feel? How do you react? Do you take it personally and go on the defensive? Do you shut down, shielding yourself from the perceived criticism?

How about when the boot's on the other foot, when others say things you disagree with. Can you be curt and dismissive? Perhaps you pull back from a potential conflict for fear of offending someone or not wanting emotions to escalate. These are two understandable reactions, but they come at a cost.

Stratospheric leaders work to master the art of having the crucial conversations that none of us enjoy, so how do we learn to have better conversations to reach better decisions without discord? It's about a change of mindset from a place of certainty to one of curiosity.

What can we learn from stratospheric leaders?

Ahead of the crucial conversation:

- **It starts with you…** Ask yourself, 'What emotional baggage might I be bringing into this conversation? What past wrongs might I be subconsciously trying to right? What stories might I be telling myself about the other person/ people? What assumptions might I be making?'

- **…and then them.** Ask yourself, 'How might they be seeing the situation? What might they know that I don't? What other perspectives might there be?'

During the conversation:

- **Stick to the facts.** No generalisations or interpretations.

- **Don't be contrary for the sake of it.** If you disagree with the other person/people, you need to offer an alternative point of view.

- **Show empathy and respect** by active listening. Listen to understand, not to reload.

- **Consider the behaviours you need to flex** to remain as the adult in the room.

- **Check in on the role that you are taking.** Has it shifted? Are you now trying to win an argument, make yourself look good or save face rather than get to the best decision for everyone?

- **When emotion runs high, intellect runs low.** Recognise when a pause or revisiting the conversation would be in service to all parties.

Applying the learning

- If you're putting it off, what are the losses and costs of not having the crucial conversation?

- Is your argument clear and specific enough?

- How can you stop yourself from being emotionally triggered by an argumentative colleague?

The intangible quality of all high-performing teams

Trust is the bedrock upon which the happiest marriages are built. It's the intangible quality that makes friendships work and it's the glue that binds high-performing teams. It's how great brands create loyalty and how companies attract and retain the best people.

Building trust doesn't happen quickly or by chance. It is created over time and by design through your words and actions.

Imagine every relationship you build as a bridge between you and another person. A bridge requires a strong foundation and in the case of relationships, the foundation is trust. Once trust is in place, it pays back in multiples in your team's effectiveness, their motivation and commitment, and this is where you experience the powerful step change from leadership to followership.

The question is, how can you build trust effectively and make it last?

What can we learn from stratospheric leaders?

- **Deliver on your promises.** Nothing builds trust as well as doing exactly what you say you will, without fail. If you won't deliver, don't make the promise.

- **Be sincere with praise.** Never underestimate the impact of a compliment or a show of appreciation.

- **Clarity matters.** Be specific in your communication. Transparency is equity.

- **Be consistent and ensure your behaviour and words align.** It avoids second guessing, watercooler chatter and ambiguity.

- **Be thoughtful in your actions.** Trust takes years to cultivate, but it can easily be broken by a hastily written email, harshly delivered feedback, an abrasive comment. These actions can change the perception of you in a heartbeat and damage a relationship forever.

- **Be authentic.** Authenticity is a superpower. We as humans are drawn to genuine people. This doesn't mean you have to share and disclose everything about yourself. It does mean demonstrating you are human and saying what you mean while meaning what you say.

- **Be humble.** Be open to disclosing what you don't know and be willing to learn from those around you.

- **Avoid fear of finding out** (**FOFO**)**.** Be curious with your colleagues and take a listening approach.

Applying the learning

- How aligned are your actions and behaviours with your words?

- How would others describe your communication style?

- When was the last time you gave sincere praise to a colleague?

Don't be the chatterbox

Lance Uggla says, 'You have two ears, one mouth. Listen twice as much as you speak.' Attentive listening is an essential skill for a stratospheric leader.

Have you ever been deep in conversation with a person when they divert their eye contact to read something on their phone? Can you recall a time where you were sharing something you perceived to be of value and the other person tried to top you with a better story of their own? Have you been on a Zoom call and as you are speaking, you can see that the other person is reading an incoming email or Slack message?

With the backdrop of busyness and needing to get things done at speed, poor listening has become a feature in many calls and meetings. Leaders can be so focused on getting to a decision quickly, they're finishing sentences, they're thinking ahead, and a lot of times they miss a whole bunch of valuable information. For the others in the room, it can invoke irritation and frustration.

Stratospheric CEOs collectively describe attentive listening as a superpower and a skill they have deliberately cultivated over time. They recognise the positive impact it makes to the outcome of a conversation. Put simply, good listeners get good insight.

What can we learn from stratospheric leaders?

- **Be conscious of being that which you want to appear.** If you want to be perceived as a good listener, you have to show you are in your words and your non-verbals.

- **Listening is an active behaviour, not a passive response.** It needs to be intentional. The quality of your listening will determine the quality of the other person's thinking.

- **Engaged listening is a sign of respect and good manners.**

- **Listen to learn.** Be curious. Ask questions. You will gain a greater understanding.

- *Listen* **and** *silent* **are anagrams of each other.** Silent doesn't simply mean being quiet. It means being still – using connected listening, eye contact and non-verbal signals that confirm you are engaged, open body language to encourage the other person to speak freely.

- **Listening is not only about the words.** There are cues and messages in the energy and sentiment behind how the words are expressed.

- **It is not those with the biggest titles and roles who always have the best ideas.** Listen to all voices in an organisation. You don't know where the best ideas may come from.

- **Set the rules of engagement in a meeting to minimise interference.** For example, 'phones away'. Your phone in particular does a great job of diluting your quality of presence.

- **Speak only when you have something valuable to say.** Crucial insights will be missed if you dominate the conversation.

- **Why am I talking (WAIT)?** If you tend to speak a lot in meetings, remember this acronym.

In Zen, it's said that it is the space between the bars that holds the tiger. In music, it is the space between the notes that creates the melody. Be intentional with your listening and see what creativity unfolds in others, and what creative dots it connects for you too.

Applying the learning

- Do you tend to speak more in meetings than others? Remember: WAIT?

- Are you always the first to answer or give an opinion?

- How good a listener are you *really?* If you were to ask your teams for feedback, what would they be sharing?

Culture And Values

Before we head into the key insights from Chapter Six, let's recall what our stratospheric leaders shared about culture and values:

- **Act on what you say.** For the stratospheric leader, their entire organisation operates on a bedrock of unwavering principles – ones that are not just words, but living and breathing standards. These standards are measured and individuals held to account.

- **Collaboration creates collective cultures.** Collaboration plays out in the flat organisational structure that actively welcomes opinions and encourages people to express their views and input into key decisions. This is critical when you are seeking to transform and disrupt. The best insights can come from anywhere in the organisation.

- **Integrity and transparency are foundations of a trust culture.** Inclusive environments build trust, which is the lifeblood of any organisation, but there are layers to trust. It firstly needs to be latticed across and within teams, which then builds the institutional trust.

- **Accessible leadership and active, honest communication.** A big ask of leaders in today's world is that they are personable, which is great for those to whom it comes naturally. For those who find it more challenging, I advise them to be accessible. That is a behaviour that can be managed.

- **Perpetuating a culture.** Once you have established the business's culture and are living it, you need to hire people to fit. Stratospheric leaders recognise that culture is a living organism.

- **A company's culture will always be defined by its worst-tolerated behaviour.** Any form of bad behaviour will undermine and corrode the company culture. Leaders must be focused on preserving the business's core values.

- **Ongoing culture cultivation.** The best way to assess culture is to listen to how your employees are describing the organisation and the environment. They will see things that you don't.

- **A good culture can help you survive a bad strategy.** It's important to continue to get smarter by fostering a culture of safety, creating an environment where people will tell the truth.

- **Don't get stuck in an echo chamber.** You don't want to look around the room and see your mirror image, nor do you want an echo chamber where you only hear your words coming back. Echo chambers are comfortable, but self-limiting.

Does leading with kindness get results?

Kindness. Kindness. Kindness. This word came up consistently when I was speaking to someone who worked at JP Morgan:

> 'He checks in on how his people really are, he remembers the finer details about your family, he knows the names and takes an interest in the receptionist/security staff. He noticed an assistant on the floor hadn't been in the office for a week and asked one of his team to check that she was OK.'

The list went on and on. These same employees expressed how they will 'take the hill' for him, because they feel part of something. They feel seen, heard, appreciated and that they matter to the organisation. His human-centric style of leadership and his warmth influence, inspire, motivate and foster loyalty. The kind of loyalty that gets results.

What you send out comes back. It's important to highlight that kindness doesn't mean being soft. In today's highly competitive high-performance business environment, you can be both kind and a strong leader, empathetic and at the same time decisive and focused. To put it another way, you can be a modern-day leader for modern-day times.

What can we learn from stratospheric leaders?

- **Empathy and compassion matter.** They can move people's worlds and the smallest gesture can have the biggest impact.

- **Acknowledge, recognise and give credit where it is deserved.** Don't miss a powerful motivational opportunity.

- **Kindness comes in many forms.** It's the way you speak, the language you use, the non-verbal communication you display, the feedback you give, the mindset you have, the judgement you don't leap to.

- **Kindness has to be authentic.** It cannot be manufactured – people will see straight through you if you fake it, directly influencing how much they trust you.

- **Kindness is contagious.** Even a small act creates a ripple effect, leaving a legacy that can be larger than you.

Applying the learning

- If kindness and empathy win trust and loyalty, what act of kindness can you offer somebody today?

Culture trumps strategy

In a conversation with a senior leader, I wanted to know what differentiates his organisation from the competition. His response? 'We are a firm that acts with integrity.' This immediately sounded like an oft-quoted cliché decorating many a corporate reception wall, so I asked for an example of integrity in action.

He described a recent deal, to date the biggest the firm had been involved in, where he had shaken hands with the counterparty. Before the paperwork could be raised, a third party came in with a bigger offer.

He consulted his leadership team members for guidance. They asked him the question, 'What do you want to do?'

He replied, 'I want to honour my handshake.'

'Then so do we,' they responded.

Stratospheric leaders are consistent and intentional about company culture. They understand short-term profits shouldn't come at the expense of long-term relationships. They start with a foundation of values, upon which everything is built, *and* they recognise the leadership team has to live and breathe them. Leaders set the tone.

What can we learn from stratospheric leaders?

- **A culture is created by people** and everybody in a company plays a vital part in creating and perpetuating that culture.

- **Create an environment where being open about, and learning from, mistakes is the norm**, not the exception.

- **Be willing to hire, appraise and fire against your company's core values.** Do behaviours within your team exemplify the culture or undermine it?

- *Kaizen* **is the Japanese philosophy of continuous improvement.** A culture needs to be invested in daily.

- **You get culture right and talent will follow.** The A players look for an environment that aligns with their values.

- **Having a set of corporate values isn't enough.** The important part is how these values translate into everyday behaviours and decision making.

- **A company culture is only as strong as its worst tolerated behaviour.** What are you willing to let go? What needs to be addressed?

- **Leaders influence behaviour**. If, for example, the management team members preach the importance of listening, they have to actively listen themselves.

Applying the learning

- How do you make sure your organisational values are lived and breathed?

- How do you want your people to describe the organisational culture?

- What is rewarded in your organisation? What behaviours get people ahead and promoted?

Do you have a cohesive leadership team?

There is something to be gained from comparing your role as a leader to the role of the conductor of an orchestra. Both roles carry the responsibility of unifying a large group of highly individual performers towards an outstanding result as a collective, yet that collective result does not detract from the sense of achievement felt by the individual members around their own contribution.

While it might be easier with instruments than people, the challenge remains the same. How do you bring everyone in the team together to collaborate and play harmoniously, while simultaneously getting the best out of them individually?

What can we learn from stratospheric leaders?

- **Encourage ownership.** Individual performance is down to the individual – their responsibility, not yours (most of the time). You want all your performers to be self-directed, make decisions and develop a self-appreciation for their work. Ownership and accountability are key.

- **Be clear on the performance you are after.** What are you and your people looking to create/achieve as a team?

Are you brainstorming new ideas or fine-tuning old ones? Whatever it is, be explicit about the outcome as well as how you'd like to get there.

- **Diversity is fundamental.** Different backgrounds and mentalities will bring different perspectives and insights, and this is beneficial for all.

- **Make sure the mission is understood.** It is key that everyone drives towards the same thing. Have clarity and steamroller out any ambiguity. The latter causes confusion, frustration and can impact morale and motivation as people pursue different agendas.

- **It's not paradise.** Not everyone will get on all the time and that's OK. We are all humans who have challenges, moods and fatigue.

- **A leader can come with ideas, but it is for the team to come up with solutions.** Collaboration and shared ownership, rather than working to comply, will drive far greater engagement and build on the vision.

- **Never fight in front of the kids.** Healthy sparring is for behind closed doors. Friction points and individual differences in a management team should not be visible to and felt by the rest of the organisation.

- **Celebrate success as a team,** the little wins as well as the big ones.

Applying the learning

- How clear is your team on the mission? How aligned are you all? How do you know?

- Are you holding people accountable to high standards?

- What working conditions and resources are you giving to your people, to help them to thrive?

What to do with the jerk genius

If you want to understand culture in a single word, look no further than your people. It is collective character that is vital to success. Where the culture is right and everybody embodies the company's values, results follow.

No individual is bigger than the team. This should be utterly non-negotiable, but what if your star performer turns out to be a bad influence? What do you do when they threaten and undermine the company's values by their toxic behaviour? This is a dilemma many leaders face, as you want the outsized contributors, but not at the cost of your culture.

What can we learn from stratospheric leaders?

- **Don't promote the jerk genius or hold them up as an example.** Promoting them sends a message across the organisation that their behaviour is OK and accepted.

- **Don't let them manage other people.** Instead, build a *big* moat around them. [Georgie to add some more explanation, so it doesn't sound like advice to ostracise the person?]

- **Don't allow power sharing between employee and employer to get out of sync.** Where does the power reside?

- **Give candid feedback, regularly.** Don't wait for the semi-annual review.

- **Call out bad behaviour when it happens,** eg passive-aggressiveness. This type of behaviour kills innovation, collaboration and trust.

- **Is this an isolated event or is there a pattern of bad behaviour?** If it's the latter, you need to make a tough call.

- **Be mindful that people can react when under pressure.** Seek to understand what is driving their behaviour.

- **Include desired behaviour in goals and objectives.** Ensure there are consequences for doing things right/wrong.

- **Look for early warning signs and wean the big egos out quickly.** If they operate from a place of 'I' versus 'we', that is always a red flag.

- **Gauge the level of toxicity.** Culture is defined by the company's worst tolerated behaviour. How is this behaviour affecting yours?

Applying the learning

- What is your organisation rewarding?

- What can you do to support the individual to ameliorate their bad behaviour?

- How honest and real time is the feedback you are giving?

What is trust?

Trust is practised over and over. It's a learned behaviour. In the end, it's the competence, confidence and cooperation that builds the muscle memory. Each of the people in the team needs to have the competence and confidence in each other, and then the ability and desire to want to cooperate.

Toto Wolff (Mercedes Formula 1 team principal and CEO) (Wolff, 2019) talks about the importance of trust in high-performance teams. He specifically references the pit stop as being demonstrative of this. The pit crew trust the driver won't injure them, despite them being centimetres from a rapidly decelerating or accelerating car, and the driver trusts that the crew can swap off and on four tyres in under two seconds. A successful pit stop can be the difference between winning or not.

Put simply, trust refers to an individual's perception of taking a risk and the response his or her teammates will have to them taking that risk. Trust is present when everyone is confident that no one on the team will embarrass or punish anyone else for admitting a mistake, asking a question or offering a new idea.

What can we learn from stratospheric leaders?

- **Personal relationships are critical to success.** Trust is built on a human connection; showing vulnerability, disclosing, listening and being supportive are fundamental building blocks.

- **Trust is like oxygen.** When it's present, you are unaware of it; when it's absent, it can be incredibly damaging to the culture.

- **Transparency and openness are trust currency.** Nobody needs to second-guess what you are thinking. Authenticity will build trust quicker than perfection.

- **Do what you say.** It's not about words, it's about actions. It's easy to say nice motivational words, but trust is earned. Deliver on your promises and be consistent with your execution.

- **Authority through position is not enough to engender trust and respect**. The leader who expects people to be team players also needs to *be* a team player.

- **If you are trustworthy, this will support you in the critical conversations**. If trust exists, your people know the messaging in the conversation is truthful and waste no time trying to understand your motive.

Applying the learning

- How clear are you that everyone in your organisation is aligned with the long-term strategy?

- Be thoughtful in your messaging. Are you saying something you want to believe, or you *do* believe?

- How much time do you invest in building relationships?

Self-Leadership

This brings us to the final key learning from our stratospheric CEOs. Let's have a quick recap:

- **Make time for self-reflection.** This is a way of bolstering and harnessing your connection with yourself and processing the stuff that simply isn't serving you.

- **Build the necessary stamina for the role.** Managing your energy is one of the keys to the long game. It is likely you recognise the real danger of burnout and chronic overwhelm, yet we can all be complicit in actively creating these through our actions.

- **Family time is fuel for the bigger picture.** If you are spending huge amounts of time away from your family, building and running a business, there will be an impact and cost. Have empathy and awareness towards how those closest to you feel. Listen to their words, their signs and silent messaging.

- **Leadership is demanding.** You may underestimate how much work is involved in entrepreneurship and building new businesses, which can create strain on your relationships. Enrol your family and friends into a common clarity of expectations around the hours you will be working, the time you will be travelling and the need for forgiveness when you will inevitably be distracted.

- **Win the morning, win the day.** Stratospheric leaders create a powerful routine for first thing in the morning to set their priorities and intentions for the day. As a result, they tend to accomplish more in less time.

- **Remove the WOMBATs.** As a leader, you need to cultivate strong self-awareness to identify your poor habits, time sucks and energy vampires. Developing positive habits, and letting go of those that aren't serving you, takes time and patience. Self-reflection is critical to holding yourself accountable during this process.

- **Be wary of the perception gap.** You can have the best of intentions about how you want to be perceived, yet a big gap can exist between that and the reality experienced by others. This stresses the importance of soliciting feedback regularly to capture insight on what your people's real experience is.

- **Realistic optimism.** Your people want to see a leader who shows they can win and has the drive, resilience, fortitude and energy to do what it takes. They also want to see you are a leader who is open to learning, grows from feedback and admits when you don't know something.

- **Create a trusted tribe.** This will give you a place to have the conversations you don't get to have elsewhere, enabling you to stay grounded. The tribe should include people you trust who have your best interests at heart – friends, family members and colleagues.

Leadership is lonely

Many leaders I work with have spoken of the loneliness of leadership, but there is a discernible difference between feeling alone and physically being alone. Most modern-day leaders are surrounded by friends, family, teams, yet can still feel isolated. They are expected to be perfect in an imperfect world and there are few places where they can fully be themselves.

Human beings are biologically wired for social connections and leaders are no exception. Nobody is an island. We are meant to experience life with others. We all need a place where we can show up as ourselves to have the conversations we don't get to have elsewhere.

This is why we as leaders need a trusted tribe around us. A safe place to vent, to let loose where there are no consequences.

What can we learn from stratospheric leaders?

- **Maintain a trusted inner circle.** 'Maintain' is a verb that requires you to act. You need to identify and invest in your tribe. It won't happen by chance.

- **Be selective with the members of your trusted tribe.** It's a privileged spot. Select friends, family members, colleagues you trust and those who have your best interests at heart.

- **Be specific with the hats you need your tribe to wear.** One person may be the truth teller who won't sugar-coat reality, another the sounding board, a third the advisor who will offer guidance. Others could be your check and balance, accountability partner or simply someone who will listen.

- **It's OK not to be OK.** People can forget leaders are humans who may have aging parents, children facing difficulties at school, stress and illness. You don't have to pretend you're OK if you're not.

- **It's not healthy to bury feelings.** If you hold on to emotion/tension, it won't necessarily be visible to others, but it will be like carrying an invisible rucksack full of heavy boulders. You will be able to feel it *and* it will impact how you show up and how people experience you.

- **Have people in your inner circle who are fun.** Life is serious enough. Spend time with those who can bring levity and enjoyment. Your feelings and emotions will change positively.

Applying the learning

- How many confidants do you have?

- How many people could you really turn to in a crisis?

- Who are you sharing moments of joy with in your life?

Your body and mind need to last you a lifetime

It's interesting, isn't it? Our pet gets sick, we take them to the vet. A child is unwell, we book a doctor's appointment. Our car breaks down, we take it to the garage for maintenance. A device is low on battery, we plug it in.

Do you give yourself the same level of care? Where do *you* feature on your priority list? In my work, I often observe that for leaders, it's scarily low down.

One client continued to show up to work every day while going through intense cancer treatment; another ignored severe abdominal pains to attend an important meeting and narrowly missed their appendix rupturing; yet another, who did not have time for a doctor's appointment, later learned they had life-threatening embolisms on their lung. A client who had their vitamin D tested received a result similar to somebody who had been in captivity for a decade!

A key risk to your business is not taking care of yourself. Nobody is coming to save you. You only have one body to live in, and it and your mind need to last you a lifetime. They must be taken care of.

What can we learn from stratospheric leaders?

- **Listen to your body whispers.** Your body is always talking to you – whether it is the cold you take longer to recover from or a chronic back condition. If you don't listen to the whispers, your body will light roadside flares, which are not as easy to bounce back from.

- **Make time to be outdoors.** It's not just the vitamin D we need. Movement is medicine.

- **Know what habits are restorative or punitive to your health.** Our energy is like a bank account – the debits are OK, so long as they are offset by credits.

- **Don't let long breaks get in the way of the short breaks.** It's important to take weekends and breaks during the day. Professional athletes refer to this as quality recovery time. They know this will allow them to come back faster, fitter, stronger.

- **Review your energy gauge.** Recognise where you are trending towards burnout. Don't wait for pain or illness to stop you in your tracks.

- **Do not confuse your capability with your capacity.** Your free time is not your availability.

- **What you consume today (food/drink/news/social media) will strongly inform tomorrow's mood, experiences and trajectory.** Choose wisely!

Applying the learning

- Where do *you* feature? What would an upgrade look like?

- What bad habits are preventing you from operating from a place of balance?

- How are you complicit in creating the conditions you say you don't want?

Are your reactions helping or harming you?

You are half-way through writing an urgent email when your child asks you, for the third time, to play football with them. A team-member is scrolling on their phone while you are sharing important information in a weekly meeting. You've just finished speaking in a crowded boardroom when a colleague asks if you feel as tired as you look.

Your reaction in these situations tells its own tale. A gesture of annoyance. A flush of anger and a curt put-down. Letting a comment deflate you in an instant. A momentary lack of self-control.

A little later, back in your calm zone, you have a moment of regret. Did I *really* need to shout? Did I *really* send that email? Did I *really* care so much about what he said?

What can we learn from stratospheric leaders?

- **Emotional hijack.** In our world of busyness and pressure, our emotions can easily become hijacked and the less logical and less rational side of our brain can take over, often with results that don't serve us or others' perceptions of us. Escaping this emotional hijack in the moment isn't easy, but if we can seek to understand why we reacted the way we did, we can train ourselves to respond differently next time.

- **Changing the way you respond** and limiting any damaging behaviours could have a dramatic impact on the results you get in work and, indeed, in life.

Applying the learning

Here are some reflective questions from stratospheric leaders. Ask yourself:

- 'Why did I react that way?'

- 'Did my reaction **help** or **harm** me?'

- 'How will I feel about this situation in one hour, one week, one year?'

- 'What may I have misunderstood or be getting wrong, especially in the heat of the moment?'

- 'What would I change if I could do it again?'

- 'What could I say to myself next time that would help me think more clearly?'

Resilience is a superpower for leaders

During holiday periods, many of us like to get away, but instead of relaxing, we may be tempted to stay connected to work – dialling into calls, checking inboxes and making ourselves available for those urgent issues.

No one has infinite capacity. We all need time out and it serves us best if we can take a complete break rather than allowing work to interfere, intermittently or continuously. Rest is not time wasted, but time invested in preventing your health, creativity and energy eroding over the long term.

What can we learn from stratospheric leaders?

- **Resilience is a superpower for leaders.** Being resilient requires you to prioritise your wellbeing. If you want to be the best of the best, you have to make the decisions in service of that.

- **Half the battle is giving yourself permission to down tools.** Pro-athletes understand that it's in the recovery where the growth happens.

- **Get clear on what rest facilitates in your life** – the impact it has on your relationships, mental clarity and decision making.

- **Be clear on what rest looks like for you** – is it exercising, sleeping, reading, listening to an audiobook, being at the beach with your children?

- **Set an intention for your break from work** to give it salience and the genuine priority it deserves. How would you like to feel at the end of your break? What would you like to do with your time? Then consider the choices you are making with regards to your answers.

- **Articulate your boundaries around availability and communication.** If you need to check in with work while on your break, carefully choose how often and the time of day that works best for you, and give yourself permission to adjust your response times.

Applying the learning

- If you are always on, what are you modelling to others?

- What permission slip do you need to give yourself with regards to rest?

- What does rest look like to you?

Thriving versus surviving

Nobody shares with you at business school just how challenging leadership can sometimes feel. At work, your people look to you for certainty, clarity and confidence in a rapidly changing and uncertain world. The demands and expectations from stakeholders can feel unrelenting. Meanwhile, at home you may be dealing with aging parents, your own health issues and challenging teens, all the while trying to figure out your how-to playbook.

You are only human. You may be an extraordinary and inspiring leader, but you also have feelings and fears. There are days where you will move mountains and there are days you will feel drained and drowning. You may even be asking yourself, 'Is it me, or are the good days feeling fewer and further between?'

How do you thrive as opposed to simply survive as a leader in today's world?

What can we learn from stratospheric leaders?

- **Nobody is an island.** Have your trusted outlets and actively use them. We all need a place where we can vent and offload, *and* a trusted team of people who have expertise in the things we don't.

- **Be on your own priority list.** A polite no is OK; placing others' priorities above your own has yet to be found in a job description.

- **Work expands so as to fill the time available for its completion** (Parkinson, 1955). Make time for the people and things that energise you.

- **Exercise self-modulation.** You can't sprint a marathon. It's stamina you will require to have sustainability in the leader's seat.

- **It's OK to b*tch, moan and whine (BMW).** Everybody has bad days, but when you do BMW, boundary the time and don't get stuck there.

- **Invest in me time.** Even a small amount of time each day or week doing something that you enjoy can have a disproportionately positive effect on your energy and outlook.

- **The joy of missing out (JOMO).** You don't have to be involved in everything, so be discerning and get conscious about your choice making.

Applying the learning

- How aware are you when you are entering into the energy red zone and the place of diminishing returns?

- How much grace and compassion do you give to yourself? Would you speak to a friend or family member the same way you speak to yourself?

- What pay-off might you gain if you chose to make quality time for yourself?

Be receptive to feedback

Stratospheric leaders understand that getting feedback is important, both in realising our potential and understanding our blind spots. They also know that asking for feedback is an excellent way to establish an environment of trust and psychological safety, which is where high performance lives.

It's not always easy, though. Asking for feedback can run counter to our need for acceptance, which was once a human survival mechanism so runs deep. Personal criticism can easily trigger a threat response, putting us into defensive mode. When we think our professionalism is being questioned or our credibility undermined, it is tempting to make excuses and blame others.

What can we learn from stratospheric leaders?

- **Ask for specifics**. Vague feedback is not helpful.

- **Solicit regular anonymous 360° feedback** to break bad habits and to learn more effective ones. Ask, 'What is *one* thing I could do differently to be a more effective leader?'

- **Get feedback in real time,** allowing for small course corrections as you go, while placing less burden on colleagues.

- **Be mindful of the polished apple.** As a leader, you won't always hear the true story. Look for the truth tellers.

- **Feedback is not eternal judgement,** and you don't have to accept it. Don't take feedback from somebody you wouldn't get advice from.

- **Create a learn-it-all not a know-it-all culture** – an environment of open feedback loops where people can confront you.

- **Listen with intent to understand.** Don't get defensive.

- **Reward your colleagues for giving feedback.** The best way to get more feedback is to show appreciation for it and work to address it.

- **Don't let your ego get in the way.** If you have a heartbeat, you have blind spots.

Applying the learning

Regarding feedback, ask yourself:

- 'People struggle to speak truth to power, so how am I actively soliciting feedback?'

- 'What could I do or stop doing that would make it easier to work with me?'

- 'What went well and what should I do more of next time?'

Happiness equals wealth

Reaching levels of extraordinary success requires grit, determination and drive, copious amounts of perseverance and an abundance of self-belief. Stratospheric leaders have learned through the arc of their journey the importance of prioritising the activities and people that mean the most to them.

What can we learn from stratospheric leaders?

- **Spend time with the people who light you up.** This is a key contributing factor to a successful, fulfilling career. Find the people who will unlock your creativity, strategic thinking and sense of fun.

- **Have clear boundaries.** Protect your yeses and make time for what matters most. Where are your boundaries blurred? Where are you overextending yourself?

- **It is possible to deliver results without sacrificing time with your family.** What are the unconscious decisions you are making that don't serve you? Your family and friends will be giving you signals, both verbal and non-verbal, if you are neglecting them. You just need to choose to listen.

- **Make sustainable productivity a focus of your leadership discussions.** Judgement and thinking are enhanced when people make time to unplug and rest. What permission do you need to give your people to have sustained success? What do you need to model?

- **Wellbeing and balance are unique to each individual.** Know which energy buckets you need filled. Energy that goes into things that don't matter comes at the expense of those that do.

Applying the learning

- Where in your life are you sacrificing your happiness?

- Your wellbeing is whispering to you all the time. If you ignore the whispers, it will ignite roadside flares to get your attention. Where are you ignoring the messages?

- Where are you taking your happiness for granted?

- Spending time with people you truly like can be part of your competitive edge. How often are you doing so?

Keep your focus where it matters

There has never been a greater demand for our time, attention, energy and focus. Staying laser-focused on the important things is one of the biggest challenges for today's leaders, given the many competing demands. Being able to effectively apportion time to the activities that matter is a skill that marks out stratospheric leaders.

How masterful are you at rationing your time and attention? How do you ensure you are investing both wisely?

What can we learn from stratospheric leaders?

- **Test commitment.** If others want your time, check how invested they are. Ask them to be explicit about how they want to use it. Curate your time and invest it where there is the likelihood of the greatest impact.

- **Set boundaries and articulate them.** While it is important to exert control over your time, it is imperative to carve out space for reflection to inform your big-picture view.

- **Empower your people to make decisions.** They shouldn't have to run everything by you. Micromanaging is disenfranchising and a waste of everyone's time.

- **If you are saying yes to something, what are you saying no to?** No is a decision; yes is a responsibility. If you can't eliminate a task, delegate it.

- **A polite no is OK** and offering a reason or an excuse is not necessary. Reasoning opens the door to the requestor wanting to negotiate.

- **Preparation, preparation, preparation.** A leader I work with uses the analogy of a book club. You wouldn't rock up and read the first chapter of the book together. Always prepare – the meeting is for discussion and decision making, not catching up on the fly.

- **Remove the WOMBATs.** Take out the calendar entries that are a waste of money, brains and time. Energy is currency.

Applying the learning

- How do you make space in your diary for preparation and getting clear in your mind your intention and purpose for the time ahead?

- What sort of impression do you make if you show up unprepared and bouncing in from another meeting? If you believed that better preparation (both material and mindset) would increase your performance and impact, what would you do differently?

Conclusion

My desire for this book is to share what I have had the privilege to learn: powerful leadership lessons from our stratospheric CEOs on _how_ they have created their success.

I'm not suggesting you go all out with the intention of matching them; rather, I want you to bear in mind their insights while you create and realise your own ambitions.

Making change is rarely about the large pronouncements and grand gestures; it is about the incremental steps that are taken, each one designed to move forward with purpose and vision. Transformation starts with the idea, but it is usually multiple years if not decades in the execution. Throughout this journey, it is the underlying drive, ferocity of vision and demonstration of the incremental successes that fuel the momentum of change.

The information and experiences in this book will likely resonate with each of you differently, which is intentional. The lessons, advice, guidance are not intended to be prescriptive, more thought provoking and inspiring, and as such they should always be mapped to your own realities, both personal and professional. No one can know you or your life better than you, so I invite you to tailor, refine and modify anything that you have read.

The only uniform statement that I will be bold enough to make is don't wait. There is never an optimal time to make the changes that you want, wish or hope for. Only you have the power to take that step as ultimately you are the conscious creator of your journey. Trust your instincts, have courage, have fortitude and be prepared for the intensities of the experience.

Onwards and upwards to the stratosphere!

Appendix:
Standout Quotes

Below, in no particular order, is a selection of quotes that really stood out for me in my conversations with the stratospheric leaders and catalysed my own thinking. I invite you to reflect on what comes up as you read them. What sparks you? What catches your attention? Where could you act?

'Raise the bar. That to me is a gold standard way of saying, "I want everything to be incrementally better."'

Lance Uggla

'If it ain't broke, break it. Push the edges and don't let the world get narrower. There is always room for continuous improvement.'

Henry Fernandez

'You are only a manager and not an entrepreneur if you don't bring down the big picture into small decisions as to what you are going to do tomorrow.'

Henry Fernandez

'There's no point in surrounding yourself with people who always agree with you. You may as well draw their salary and agree with yourself.'

Michael Spencer

'Entrepreneurs have an unshakable belief that they'll find a way. You can't be an entrepreneur if you're a pessimistic person. It requires so much belief that you will figure it out.'

Henry Fernandez

'There are people who got lucky, but if you really examine all the decisions, the way they got there, it's not luck. It was a set of attitudes that got them there.'

Lee Olesky

'You have got to dream where you are going. If you dream you are going to go up three steps, you'll get up three steps, but why not dream you are going to go to the top?'

Lance Uggla

'You want to be in the business of problems looking for solutions, not solutions looking for problems.'

Henry Fernandez

'No idea starts big, and you have to start somewhere. The question is, is the idea scalable?'

Henry Fernandez

'The recipe for business creation is extremely simple. You have to put yourself in the shoes of others and see the world from their perspective, from their angle. What is the unmet need?'

Henry Fernandez

'Never behave as if or assume that you are the most intelligent man in the room. Surround yourself with super smart people.'

Michael Spencer

'I never lose sleep over taking a risky decision. If you want to move fast, you have got to make decisions to allow things to keep moving.'

Lance Uggla

'Why do 95% of new businesses fail? It's because they run out of money. You never know what icebergs you are going to run into, so always raise more money than you think you need.'

Rick McVey

'The best education is the one that develops the brain and refines the instinct. You need to learn how to build your analytical skills, and then you need to learn to let your instincts go wild.'

Henry Fernandez

'Don't do too many things. Less is more. Focus on one or two ideas. Don't focus on five to ten because inevitably, you don't have the capability to execute at that level.'

Lance Uggla

'Carpe diem, seize the opportunity. It's a sacred motto and it's one of those things a lot of people don't do.'

Lance Uggla

'As a leadership team, you all need to be rowing together. Otherwise you will really be diminished in what you can achieve as a group.'

Michael Spencer

'Embrace failure. The chance that every idea you have is a good one is zero. Be brave enough to have lots of ideas, and accept that many won't succeed. It will enable you to uncover the killer ones.'

Chris Willcox

'Many people spend all their time on strategy, but execution is everything. You go to business school and 70% of your lessons are on strategy and 5% on execution. If you can't execute, you don't have anything.'

Lance Uggla

'Any idea without execution is worth nothing. An OK idea with great execution is worth a lot. That is why getting things done, getting them done well, getting them done on time, on budget and course correcting where needed is really the lifeblood of business.'

Rick McVey

'The lessons from failure are the seeds of success. Hands down a hundred to one, failures are more important than successes. I sometimes don't even remember the successes I have had. I remember every failure and if you are smart, you analyse or confront them and you turn them upside down.'

Lee Olesky

'Most of the lessons from my failures are common sense that wasn't that common.'

Henry Fernandez

'The ones that can combine strategic long-term thinking with rigorous execution year in and year out are rare people.'

Rick McVey

'Luck makes a difference. If you have bad luck, it's incredibly difficult to have a victory. Bad luck is a test. However, the difference is knowing when it was bad luck vs when you made a mistake.'

Michael Spencer

'Regularly assess the skills you need around the table. Ask yourself, "What skills are we missing?"'

Rick McVey

'What made you successful can also be what causes you to fail. As you ascend, you will need different skills and a different style.'

Chris Willcox

'Work around the doubters. Leverage the believers.'

Rick McVey

'Any innovative or new business is going to have its share of failures, even when all the homework has been done. We learn lessons from the failures, but we do not dwell on them. Most importantly, don't be afraid of them.'

Rick McVey

'A crisis is a terrible thing to waste.'

Henry Fernandez

'If you're a business owner, you know the difficult times will come. It's just a question of when, so you have to be prepared for them.'

Henry Fernandez

'Being positive is infectious. It fuels you. The cup-half-empty person just drains life out of a room.'

Lance Uggla

'You have two ears, one mouth. Listen twice as much as you speak. You can learn something from every conversation.'

Lance Uggla

'If you are in a customer business, the customers work out over time whether you are a person who is reliable and consistent. If you play honestly with your clients over the long term, it will pay off.'

Michael Spencer

'Leadership really is a fortunate position to be in and therefore, you need to find ways to keep lifting people up.'

Lance Uggla

'It's important as a leader to make decisions and then take responsibility for them, right or wrong. It's an essential talent to be able to admit if you've made a bad decision or to take responsibility for approving a bad decision.'

Chris Willcox

'I build support around me to allow me to operate at the highest possible level. I trust the people around me, which ultimately saves me a lot of time.'

Lance Uggla

'Leadership is about taking people where they do not yet know they need to go.'

Lance Uggla

'I don't want to give you the fish. I'd rather give you the fishing rod.'

Henry Fernandez

'Leadership is not about you. Leadership is about the people that follow you.'

Chris Willcox

'You have a responsibility to the opportunity – to the seat you sit in.'

Henry Fernandez

'There are a lot of people who hire great talent and make the decisions for them. You have to empower your people and allow them to do what they need to do, and *don't* get in their way.'

Henry Fernandez

'There is not one single path to success. A different way of doing things can lead to the same high-quality output.'

Henry Fernandez

'None of us get very far on our own.'

Rick McVey

'The leader sets the tone for everyone else. You have to be a bit of a contrarian. When things are going poorly, you need to be the most optimistic, and when things are going great, you need to remind people that you are not as good as you think you are.'

Rick McVey

'You don't want to create walls, but you also don't want your day consumed with one-on-one conversations. Be intentional at managing and protecting your time.'

Rick McVey

'Be curious. Actively learn from others. You always want to be broadening your thinking.'

Chris Willcox

'I think empathy is a huge component to leadership. I think if you can really put yourself in the other person's shoes and try to understand what their objectives are, it helps build trust, which is critical to relationships.'

Lee Olesky

'As a leader, it is important to let go of any self-imposed expectations to have all the answers. A big part of being a leader is bringing other people into the problem solving.'

Chris Willcox

'Without trust, you don't have a long-term sustainable business in any field.'

Chris Willcox

'It's important to continue to get smarter by fostering a culture of safety, creating an environment where people will tell the truth.'

Chris Willcox

'The more you can create an open culture, the less watercooler secrets there are.'

Henry Fernandez

'In hiring, evidence of teamwork trumps all else. Look for culture carriers in every candidate.'

Henry Fernandez

'Manners matter. It's a sign of respect.'

Lance Uggla

'Have an above-average work ethic. Work ethic is a way of life. To create amazing success, you are going to have to work harder than 99% of the people you know.'

Lance Uggla

'You have got to be prepared to change what you have done in the past, to do what you're going to do in the future.'

Michael Spencer

'Make sure you distribute your energy across all aspects of your life. Find some downtime for relaxing, exercise and eating well. All those things are really fuel to the bigger picture.'

Lance Uggla

'You are your choices and actions.'

Chris Willcox

'My philosophy in life is the power of compounding. What matters is consistency.'

Henry Fernandez

'Almost all the time, you're on the line. You're always experiencing some level of self-doubt. The important thing is, how do you balance out the doubts versus the conviction?'

Henry Fernandez

'Think long and hard about what your priorities are in life and be on a path that's going to ultimately make you really happy longer term.'

Rick McVey

'Make time for your mental outlet – whether it is sleep or sports – and take vacations when you need them. It's part of creating long-term performance. Physical fitness does feed into mental fitness.'

Rick McVey

'One of my biggest faults and maybe also a positive is that I don't spend a lot of time celebrating success. I'm always looking for what the next thing is. Don't miss a valuable opportunity to motivate those around you.'

Lance Uggla

'It's OK to disagree, just don't be disagreeable.'

Rick McVey

References

Meet Our CEOs

Canal, E, '30 inspiring quotes from amazing athletes and coaches', *Forbes* (22 April, 2016), www.forbes.com/sites/emilycanal/2016/04/22/30-inspiring-quotes-from-amazing-athletes-and-coaches, accessed 9 July 2024

Machiavelli, N, *The Prince* (Antonio Blado d'Asolo, 1532; Reader's Literary Classics, 2021)

Part One

One: An Audacious Vision

Collins, J and Porras, JI, *Built to Last: Successful habits of visionary companies* (William Collins, 1994)

Covey, S, *The 4 Disciplines of Execution: Achieving your wildly important goals* (Simon & Schuster, 2015)

History.com Editors, 'Manifest Destiny' (Sky History, 2019), www.history.com/topics/19th-century/manifest-destiny, accessed 12 February 2024

Two: Risk Is Possibility

Synnott, M, *The Impossible Climb: Alex Honnold, El Capitan and the climbing life* (Allen & Unwin, 2019)

Yerkes, RM and Dodson, JD, 'The relation of strength of stimulus to rapidity of habit-formation', *Journal of Comparative Neurology and Psychology*, 18 (1908), pp459–82, http://dx.doi. org/10.1002/cne.920180503

Three: Execution

Brinkman, A, 'Slow is smooth and smooth is fast', Amanda Brinkman Blog (24 July 2019), https://amandakbrinkman.com/ slow-is-smooth-and-smooth-is-fast, accessed 14 March 2023

Newton, I, *Philosophiae Naturalis Principia Mathematica* (Mathematical Principles of Natural Philosophy, 1687)

Sinek, S, *Start with Why: How great leaders inspire everyone to take action* (Penguin 2011)

Four: Global Crisis Management

Goldsmith, H, *What Got You Here Won't Get You There: How successful people become even more successful* (Profile Books, 2008)

Lee, H, *To Kill a Mockingbird* (Arrow, 2010; first published 1960)

Shapiro, J, 'How Shakespeare's great escape from the plague changed theatre', *The Guardian* (24 September 2015), www. theguardian.com/books/2015/sep/24/shakespeares-great- escape-plague-1606--james-shapiro, accessed 10 March 2023

Swindoll, C, *Life Is 10% What Happens to You and 90% How You React* (Nelson Books, 2023)

Five: Leading Others

Carnegie, D, *How to Win Friends and Influence People* (Vermilion, 2012)

Grant, A, *Hidden Potential: The science of achieving greater things* (WH Allen, 2023)

Percy, S, '9 New Year's resolutions for leaders in 2024', *Forbes* (2023), www.forbes.com/sites/sallypercy/2023/12/30/9-new-years-resolutions-for-leaders-in-2024, accessed 12 February 2024

Sinek, S, 'Customers will never love a company…', Twitter (16 April 2014), https://twitter.com/simonsinek/status/456545886143643649, accessed 10 March 2023

Six: Culture And Values

Dweck, CS, *Mindset: Changing the way you think to fulfil your potential* (Robinson, 2017)

Velumyan, N, 'Global change and the role of business identity', *Forbes* (14 December 2021), www.forbes.com/sites/forbescoachescouncil/2021/12/14/global-change-and-the-role-of-business-identity, accessed 9 March 2023

Seven: Self-Leadership

B2B Marketing, 'Half the money I spend on advertising is wasted; the trouble is I don't know which half' (B2B, 2015), https://b2bmarketing.net/archive/half-the-money-i-spend-on-advertising-is-wasted-the-trouble-is-i-dont-know-which-half-b2b-marketing-2, accessed 12 February 2024

Bartlett, S (@StevenBartlett) 'There is no self-development without self-awareness…', Twitter (30 September 2020), https://twitter.com/StevenBartlett/status/1311331455017062406?lang=en, accessed 12 February 2024

Bezos, J, 'We are our choices', YouTube (2018), www.youtube.com/watch?v=3fv3nX-I5KU, accessed 12 February 2024

Dweck, CS, *Mindset: Changing the way you think to fulfil your potential* (Robinson, 2017)

Eurich, T, *Insight: How to succeed by seeing yourself clearly* (Pan Books, 2018)

Gallwey, WT, *The Inner Game of Golf* (Pan, 2015)

Nadella, S, 'The learn-it-all leader does better than the know-it-all leader', *Wall Street Journal* video (23 January 2019), www.wsj.com/video/satya-nadella-the-learn-it-all-does-better-than-the-know-it-all/D8BC205C-D7F5-423E-8A41-0E921E86597C, accessed 13 February 2024

Shot Scope, *The Ultimate Golfer's Guide: Free e-book on lowering your scores* (2023), https://shotscope.com/uk/golf-ebooks/ultimate-golfers-guide, accessed 13 March 2023

Tollin, M, *The Last Dance* (Netflix, 2020)

Part Two

Lessons: Two – Risk Is Possibility

Levy, I, 'Who has missed the most shots in NBA history?' *Fansided* (2021), https://fansided.com/2021/08/26/kobe-bryant-most-missed-shots-nba-history, accessed 9 March 2023

Lessons: Three – Execution

Sudeikis, J, Lawrence, B, Hunt, B and Kelly, J, 'Apple unveils first look at new original comedy series *Ted Lasso*, starring Jason Sudeikis' (Apple TV+ press release, 2020), www.apple.com/tv-pr/news/2020/05/apple-unveils-first-look-at-new-original-comedy-series-ted-lasso-starring-jason-sudeikis, accessed 5 February 2024

Lessons: Five – Global Crisis Management

Kosinski, J (director); E Kruger, E Warren Singer, C McQuarrie (writers) *Top Gun: Maverick* (Paramount, 2022)

Swindoll, C, *Life Is 10% What Happens to You and 90% How You React* (Nelson Books, 2023)

Lessons: Six – Culture And Values

Wolff, T, *Gareth Southgate: How to lead with Toto Wolff* (Channel 4, 2019), www.channel4.com/programmes/gareth-southgate-how-to-lead-with-toto-wolff, accessed 5 February 2024

Lessons: Seven – Self-Leadership

Parkinson, CN, 'Parkinson's Law', *The Economist* (1955), www.economist.com/news/1955/11/19/parkinsons-law, accessed 15 February 2024

Recommended Reading

Bariso, J, *EQ Applied: The real-world guide to emotional intelligence* (Borough Hall, 2018)

Collins, J, *Good To Great: Why some companies make the leap... and others don't* (Random House Business, 2001)

Covey, S, *The 7 Habits of Highly Effective People* (Simon & Schuster, 2020)

Duckworth, A, *Grit: Why passion and resilience are the secrets to success* (Vermilion, 2017)

Dweck, C, *Mindset: Changing the way you think to fulfil your potential* (Robinson, 2017)

Epstein, D, *Range: How generalists triumph in a specialized world* (Macmillan, 2020)

Ferriss, T, *Tribe of Mentors: Short life advice from the best in the world* (Vermilion, 2017)

Fogg, BJ, *Tiny Habits: The small changes that change everything* (Virgin Books, 2019)

Goldsmith, M, *What Got You Here Won't Get You There: How successful people become even more successful* (Generic, 2013)

Masters, B and Thiel, P, *Zero to One: Notes on startups, or how to build the future* (Virgin Books, 2015)

Schmidt, E, Rosenberg, J and Eagle, A, *Trillion Dollar Coach: The leadership playbook of Silicon Valley's Bill Campbell* (John Murray, 2020)

Schwarzman, S, *What It Takes: Lessons in the pursuit of excellence* (Avid Reader Press/Simon & Schuster, 2019)

Sieger, R, *Natural Born Winners: How to achieve your ambitions and create the success you want* (Birkhall Media, 2012)

Stanier Bungay, M, *The Coaching Habit: Say less, ask more and change the way you lead forever* (Page Two, 2016)

Thorndike, WN, *The Outsiders: Eight unconventional ceos and their radically rational blueprint for success* (Harvard Business Review Press, 2012)

Webb, C, *How to Have a Good Day: The essential toolkit for a productive day at work and beyond* (Pan, 2017)

Acknowledgements

This book has been a genuine team effort, and I am eternally grateful to everyone who has shared their time, energy and expertise in its creation. In particular, I would like to thank the stratospheric founders/CEOs who not only gave me hours of their time, but trusted me to tell their stories: Henry Fernandez, Rick McVey, Lee Olesky, Michael Spencer, Lance Uggla and Chris Willcox.

I would also like to acknowledge the contributions of a number of other brilliantly talented leaders and colleagues of our CEOs who provided further context and insight for the book: Shane Akeroyd, Nancy Altobello, Mark Beeston, Richard Berliand, Chris Brindley, Stephen Casper, Chris Concannon, Mazy Dar, Tony DeLise, Craig Donaldson, Sari Granat, Carlos Hernandez, Jack Jeffrey, Adam Kansler, Will Meldrum, Kevin McPherson, Sally Moore, Yaacov Mutnikas, Emily Portney, Richie Prager, David Rutter, Rich Schiffman, Mary Sedarat, Ram Sharan, Edouard Tavernier, Gordon and Lorraine Uggla, and Daniel Yergin.

There was a small and amazing group of people who were each incredible collaborators and partners in the book's creation. Thank you to Laurie Aaron, Lawrence Bernstein, Caroline Butler, Sarah Chaplin-Lee, Simon Dickins, Klaudia Gorczyca, Patti Hall, Anna O'Kennedy, Richard Taylor, and Nicola White.

Finally, huge thanks to Someera Khokhar and Brad Levy for being my expert sounding boards throughout the project. Thank you for your patience, insight and encouragement every step of the way.

The Author

Georgie Dickins is an internationally recognised authority on leadership, sought-after speaker, author and coach. She serves as a trusted advisor to CEOs and change makers within the financial services industry and is appreciated as a modern-day leadership expert by both corporations and the industry titans that lead them alike.

Georgie's twenty years of experience in the financial services industry has given her extensive exposure to the requirements of leadership as well as the expectations placed on business leaders, enabling her to truly understand them. She is passionate about sharing insights from the top of successful organisations and has created CEO circles and mastermind groups, bringing together, incubating and inspiring the next generation of leaders, visionaries and entrepreneurs.

As the co-founder and managing director of Cajetan, a boutique firm specialising in transformational leadership, Georgie orchestrates impactful change within organisations. She is also the founder behind Women In Leadership Global, a peer network with a mission to advance the face of leadership across the world's most influential industries.

Based in Suffolk, Georgie splits her time between her home, London and New York.

🌐 www.cajetangroup.com

🌐 www.georgiedickins.com

🌐 www.womeninleadershipglobal.com

in www.linkedin.com/in/georgie-dickins-5083686a